THE RIVER

نهرالأنوار

SHAYKH FAID MOHAMMED SAID

Published by ISRA Books
Unit 4
5 Durham Yard
London E2 6QF
Israbooks.co.uk

Bismillah-ir Rahman-ir Raheem
"Allah guides to His Light whom He wills."
(Surah An-Nur: 35)

All rights reserved
First edition 2016

© Copyright 2016 Faid Mohammed Said

Faid Muhammad Said reserves the right to be acknowledged as the author of this work. All rights reserved. No part of this publication may be reproduced, stored in a retrieval system, or transmitted, in any form or by any means, without the author's prior permission

Cover Design and Calligraphy: Moustafa Hassan
Graphic Design: Mahbub Alam

Printed by Mega Printing in Turkey

Contents

Introduction	XI
Forward	XIII
In Anticipation of the Arrival of the New Year	1
Supplication in Extreme Weather	4
Munajaat: Mercy	6
Munajaat e Ishq e Rasulullah ﷺ	7
Poem of Syedina Abu Talib	11
New Year – Muharram 1, 1435	14
To The Mercy of Allah ﷻ	18
Giving	21
Do Not Lose Hope	22
Munajaat	24
Rasulullah ﷺ : The Source of all Change Towards Khair	28
Question: How do I Know if My Iman is Increasing?	33
Surah An-Nur: How to Deal and have Adab with the Nur	39
Hikmah: Ni'mah from Allah ﷻ	41
Rabi ul Awwal Mubarak	43
Poem of Al Abbas ؓ	45
Tawfiq is from Him	47
Hajj and Umrah	49
Astaghfar – Forgiveness	51
Best of Characters – Khuluqul Adheem	53
To Know Him is to be Shy	57
Jummah Mubarak – Dua	59
Rahma – After Difficulty Comes Ease	61
Shifa	62
Poem of Hafiz al Dimashqi ؓ	64
Run to Him	65
Illness and its Cure	67
Dua	69
Heart of Love	71
Beautiful Hearts	73
Wisdom	75
Does Allah Love Me?	78

In the Wisdom of Allah ﷻ	80
Wisdom	82
Good Thoughts and Reminders	84
Ramadan Mubarak	86
Shukr (Gratefulness) – Part One	88
What is Shukr (Gratefulness) – Part Two	93
Ramadan Farewell	97
Your Secret with Him	100
Husn Dhan	102
"...Say 'Allah!' and leave others to their amusement."	104
Poem of Syeda Aisha ؓ	107
The Source of Happiness	108
The Blessing of the Ten Days of Dhul Hijjah	111
Munajaat	118
Moments of Happiness: A Gift from Allah ﷻ	120
Humility	123
The Reality of Life	126
Qur'an References	129
Hadith References	130
Poem References	137
Biographical Index	145

To My Parents,

Umm Ahmad and Abu Ahmad,

Who, through their love and affection,

Gave all those who came in contact with them a drink from The River of Light,

And it is the shade of that Baraka,

That we are still living in today.

Introduction

Bismillah-ir Rahman-ir Raheem.

"Allah guides to His Light whom He wills." (Surah An-Nur)

In Surah Al-Maidah, Allah ﷻ described Rasulullah ﷺ as a Nur from Himself, and this cannot be defined or described even in it of itself.

Allah ﷻ is Nur, and we are recepients of all the *khair* from Him as He has blessed us with Rasulullah ﷺ, who is all of the Anwar! As Allah ﷻ says in Surah Ash-Shura: *"Verily, you guide to the straight path,"* speaking of Rasulullah ﷺ.

Contained herein are notes that have been written on various occasions as a reminder to ourself and our beloved brothers and sisters; as Allah ﷻ said to Rasulullah ﷺ in Surah Al-Ghashiyah (21-22): *"So remind; you are only a reminder. You are not over them a controller."*

Allah ﷻ said in another verse, *"Verily, the reminder benefits the believers."* (Surah Ad-Dhariyat, 55)

The main driver of these notes was love, and what can be said about love unless it is shared. With regards to sharing, there is nothing better than to sit together in the gathering of wisdom, as Allah ﷻ said in Surah Al-Baqarah (269): *"He gives wisdom to whom He wills, and whoever has been given wisdom has certainly been given much good."*

And Rasulullah ﷺ used to share wisdom and love with everyone.

So the purpose of these writings was not to produce a book or articles discussing specific topics in depth, but rather, what was intended to be paramount in these writings is the love for Rasulullah ﷺ, to get closer to Rasulullah ﷺ, all by sharing the *khair* we get from Rasulullah ﷺ with His *ummah*. Thus, the collection contains *ayat* of Qur'an, Hadith of

Rasulullah ﷺ and many stories of the Saliheen.

May Allah ﷻ benefit those who read it, and may He forgive those who wrote it.

May Allah ﷻ join us all with His Beloved Syedi ﷺ.

Allahumma salli alaa Nur

Faid Mohammed Said

28 Dhul Hijjah 1435

Foreword

Bismillah-ir Rahman-ir Raheem.

Allah ﷻ mentions in Surah Al-Baqarah (269): *"He gives wisdom to whom He wills, and whoever has been given wisdom has certainly been given much good. And none will understand except those of great understanding."*

It was narrated by ibn Abbas ﷺ that wisdom in the above *ayah* means *marifah* and understanding the Qur'an. Allah ﷻ said in the Qur'an in the *dua* of Syedina Ibrahim ﷺ for the ummah in Surah Al Baqarah (129): *"...send among them a messenger from themselves who will recite to them Your verses and teach them the Book and wisdom and purify them..."* Allah ﷻ is the one who inspires His servants! And as Allah ﷻ has mentioned regarding Rasulullah ﷺ in Surah Al-Anbiya (107): *"And We have not sent you except as a Mercy for all the worlds."* As such, part of that Mercy is sharing the *khair* (great benefit and blessing), which is an essential of the *deen* (religion).

In sharing Mercy, we are seeking Allah's ﷻ pleasure and in order to achieve the *dua* of Rasulullah ﷺ that is narrated in a Hadith by many Sahaba, including Abdullah ibn Masud, Zayd ibn Thabit, Muadh ibn Jabal, ibn Mutaib, Anas ibn Malik, and Abu Darda ﷺ, in at-Tirmidhi, in which Rasulullah ﷺ said: *"May Allah ﷻ bless and put Nur on those who listen to what we say, understand it, memorize it and then share it with others."*

The whole purpose of the the *deen* is sharing the *khair*.

Through these writings, our intention was to share *nasiha* related to the *deen* and daily life, and the intention was not to attempt to create a comprehensive or exhaustive piece of work on any given topic. Some brothers, with good intention, asked permission to put these writings in book form for others to benefit. Hence, we thought we should put this work together ourselves in order to share Qur'an, Hadith and stories of the Righteous.

"Say, 'This is my way; I invite to Allah with insight, I and those who follow me...'" (Surah Yusuf: 108)

Also, because writing is one of the greatest achievements of this *ummah*, as Allah ﷻ called the Qur'an "Kitab", which literally means "written." Thus, Muslims are encouraged to write. In Surah Al-Baqarah (282), Allah ﷻ mentioned that all financial transactions should be written, and, encouraged by Rasulullah ﷺ, Abdullah ibn Amr ibn Al As used to write – so keep writing!

The short Surah Al-Asr mentions that all mankind is in absolute loss except those who do good deeds, are truthful and patient.

Imam Shafi ﷺ said of this Surah, if Allah ﷻ was not to reveal other than Surah Al Asr, it was to be enough!

Four things keep us out of this loss:

1) *Iman* – the result of *marifah*. Without *iman* we are useless
2) Righteous deeds - as Allah ﷻ does not accept *iman* without deeds
3) Advise to the Truth: Share *iman* and deeds and what Allah ﷻ gives you
4) Have patience when you advise in doing good deeds.

As Allah ﷻ has given us everything, we should be pleased.

In a Hadith Qudsi, it is mentioned: *"Oh, the son of Adam! I created what is in the heavens and earth for you, so do not waste time in worrying about it, and I created you for Me, so do not lapse in fulfilling My rights. Do not waste time from what I have commanded you.*

Allah ﷻ said to Rasulullah ﷺ in Surah Al-Ghashiyah (21-22): *"You are just a reminder. We did not send you to control them."*

All that we do is just a reminder.

Faid Mohammed Said

Bismillah-ir Rahman-ir Raheem
"There has come to you from Allah a Light and a Clear Book."
(Surah Al-Maidah: 15)

In Anticipation of the Arrival of the New Year

16 Dhul Hijjah 1434 - 21 October 2013

All praise is due to Allah ﷻ, the One who purified the hearts of His righteous slaves from the control of their desires and from the menacing grip of doubts; until such moment that they became aware of His Great Ability and the Greatness of Him being the Over-Powering.

And we thank Him with the thanks of the one who acknowledges His Glory, Perfection and enjoys the sea of His Generosity and Grace.

And I bear witness that no one is worthy of worship other than the Creator of the heavens and the earth, a statement that leads the bearer to *jannah*! And I bear witness that our Master ﷺ is His Slave, Messenger, Beloved and Friend sent to all of creation, and that Rasulullah ﷺ is from the Great Signs and Miracles of Allah ﷻ, as the one who discovers knows.

Oh Allah ﷻ, send Your *salawat* upon Rasulullah ﷺ, his family, a family of the great Imams; upon His Companions, the righteous; and those who follow in their footsteps.

Dear brothers and sisters, in a few days we are to bid farewell to this year, 1434 years after the *hijrah* of the Beloved ﷺ, and as we bid farewell we welcome the start of a new year.

We ask Allah ﷻ that we end this year with His Grace (*karm*), and that the year to come be that of abundant blessings (*khair*).

At the close of this year, I have this message:

Turn the page of this year, with all its sadness, calamities and separation; we must think carefully about what has transpired over the course of this past year and extract from it a lesson. We must now climb the mountain of *tawbah* and make *istighfar* from every sin that we have committed.

We must forgive everyone who has hurt us, and forgive them with the utmost love.

We must forget that we have forgiven them, and forget for what we have forgiven.

I urge you to remember that we have a Lord ﷻ who does not leave His slaves to themselves! Whatever we go through has been ordained and written by Him ﷻ. We should be pleased with what has happened, and pleased for that which is to come.

Let us make our slogan the *ayat* of the Qur'an (Surah Al-Hadid, 23): *"Do not regret what has been missed, and do not be excited for that which we have received."*

Be pleased with the past and the future that is yet to come. Be optimistic about the future for us and the *ummah*.

The days have passed, without notice, and the new year has arrived. With every year that passes, although we do not notice, everything changes. Our feelings, emotions and we ourselves change. A lot of things happen, and a lot of memories are recorded, some painful some not.

We have no other choice but to ask Allah ﷻ with absolute confidence, and He shall give. May this be a year of blessing (*khair*), safety, love, hope and forgiveness (*maghfirah*).

I urge you to forgive each other, as we do not know how long we are to be in this *dunya*.

Forgive me for everything that I have done on purpose or by mistake, and know that I have forgiven all, and that I have nothing but feelings of love.

Please accept these few words.

Do not look back at the past, otherwise you will be hurt.

Do not look at today, or you might feel discomfort.

Do not look at the future, as you may feel depressed.

But look and have hope only in Allah ﷻ!

Because He is Ar-Rahman ur Rahim ﷻ. Let Him choose what is best for us in *dunya* and in *al akhira*.

And as Rasulullah ﷺ said: "Whoever is not thankful to the people, he is not thankful to Allah ﷻ" [*at-Tirmidhi*]. I would like to thank you very much and *jazakAllah khair* for your *Duas*, patience, condolences and for standing by us.

May Allah ﷻ gather us with Rasulullah ﷺ in *Firdaus Al A'laa*, as He has gathered us in *dunya*.

Supplication in Extreme Weather

23 Dhul Hijjah 1434 - 28 October 2013

As I always say Sayyedy صلى الله عليه وسلم life was *dua*.

So please at the time of heavy winds

Recite:

اللَّهُمَّ اجْعَلْهَا رَحْمَةً وَلَا تَجْعَلْهَا عَذَابًا ، اللَّهُمَّ اجْعَلْهَا رِيَاحًا وَلَا تَجْعَلَهَا رِيحًا

When there is a heavy wind, sit in the position of Tashahud and recite:

"O Allah, let it be a mercy and not a punishment. O Allah make it a beneficial and not a destructive wind".

Also recite

اللَّهُمَّ إِنِّي أَسْأَلُكَ خَيْرَهَا وَخَيْرَ مَا فِيهَا وَخَيْرَ مَا أُرْسِلَتْ بِهِ وَأَعُوذُ بِكَ مِنْ شَرِّهَا وَشَرِّ مَا فِيهَا وَشَرِّ مَا أُرْسِلَتْ بِهِ

Allaahumma 'innee 'as'aluka khayrahaa, wa khayra maa feehaa, wa khayra maa 'ursilat bihi wa audhu bika min sharrihaa, wa sharri maa feehaa, wa sharri maa 'ursilat bihi

"Oh Allah, I ask from you the best of the winds, the best of what is in the winds, and the best of what it brings. Oh Allah, I seek refuge from the evil of the winds, from the evil of what is in the winds, and from the evil of what it brings."

If there is a darkness with the heavy wind, recite Surah Falaq and Surah Naas.

At the time of rain
Recite:

اللَّهُمَّ صَيِّبًا نَافِعًا

Allaahumma sayyiban naafi'an
"O Allah make it plentiful and beneficial".

When rain exceeds the limits Recite:

اللَّهُمَّ حَوَالَيْنَا ، وَلَا عَلَيْنَا ، اللَّهُمَّ عَلَى الآكَامِ ، وَالظِّرَابِ ، وَبُطُونِ الأَوْدِيَةِ ، وَمَنَابِتِ الشَّجَرِ

Allaahumma hawaalaynaa wa laa 'alaynaa. Allaahumma 'alal-'aakaami wadh-dhiraabi, wa butoonil-'awdiyati, wa manaabitish-shajari

"O Allah, let it rain around us and not on us. O Allah, let it rain on the peaks and mountains and the valleys and at the forests".

At the time of thunder Recite:

اللَّهُمَّ لَا تُهْلِكْنَا بِعَذَابِكَ وَلَا تَقْتُلْنَا بِغَضَبِكَ وَعَافِنَا قَبْلَ ذَلِكَ

"O Allah, do not let us die by Your anger and do not destroy us with Your punishment, but grant us safety".

When it Thunders:

سُبْحَانَ الَّذِي يُسَبِّحُ الرَّعْدُ بِحَمْدِهِ ، وَالْمَلَائِكَةُ مِنْ خِيفَتِهِ

Subhaanal-lathee yusabbihur-ra'du bihamdihi walmalaa'ikatu min kheefatihi

"Glory is to Him Whom thunder and angels glorify due to fear of Him"

Whenever Abdullah bin Zubair ﷺ would hear thunder, he would abandon all conversation and say this supplication.

May Allah protect you and watch over you!

Munajaat: Mercy

25 Dhul Hijjah 1434 - 30 October 2013

Ya Allah ﷻ, as the end of the year approaches I remember the end of time and the Day of Judgement and in doing so remember all the things I have done and all those I did not do, by Your Grace and Giving. It is with Your Grace and Giving that I am able to recollect all that I have done and have not done. It is You who gives us everything, and You never left me, as You are my Sponsor, and You are my Helper and it is in You that we seek refuge.

Ya Rabbi, Syedi Rasulullah ﷺ told us that from the *ni'mah* (blessings) that You have Bestowed upon us, is that we do not see our blessings or our shortcomings, we only see You. On that very Day, out of Your Mercy, no one will hear our shortcomings, not even the *malaika* (angels)! On that Day You will say: Oh My slave, do you remember when you did this? Oh Allah ﷻ on that very Day You are our Sponsor, You are our Helper, and when You remind us, cover our *dunya* and allow us to forget about *akhira*; we only request that our *salawat* for Syedi Rasulullah ﷺ and *ibadah* is accepted.

We need and rely on Your *Rahma* (Mercy) to make us closer, to make us worthy of being followers of Syedi Rasulullah ﷺ. You chose us to say the *Kalima*, and You engraved it upon our hearts, and allowed us to make *dhikr* in *dunya* and *al akhira*. Do not end our existence without raising our *maqam* such that we begin, end and embody the *Kalima*.

I am but a slave, the son of a slave, the grandson of slaves. I have no will or desire for *wilayat* (sainthood), no desire to be from the *muqaribeen* (the close ones), all I want is to be accepted as Your slave and Your *Rahma*.

Allahumma salli wa sallim alaa Sayyidina Muhammad wa alaa Ahli Sayyidina Muhammad fi kulli lamhatin wa nafasin 'adada maa wa see-a-hu 'il-mullah

Munajaat e Ishq e Rasulullah ﷺ

28 Dhul Hijjah 1434 - 2 November 2013

Oh my heart you are blessed by the love of Muhammad ﷺ, and blessed that this love has been made *fard* on you by Allah ﷻ.

Our love for him ﷺ is likened to humble gratitude, the greatest *ni'mah* from Allah ﷻ, which is renewed every second. Indeed this is the Greatest Gift of Allah ﷻ.

Such a Gift, that brings guidance to all.

A guidance that Khalil ﷺ asked for.

A glad tiding of Isa ﷺ, which he constantly prayed for.

Seal of all the Prophets, the Seal of Taqwa, the Seal of the great slaves of Allah ﷻ, who worshipped and implemented *tawheed*.

He is the last, the one under which all with gather, the purity, the perfection; He is Ahmad ﷺ.

All the messengers, are but his followers ﷺ.

If you want to follow with them, Allah ﷻ said:

And when Allah took the covenant of the prophets, "Whatever I give you of the Scripture and wisdom and then there comes to you a messenger confirming what is with you, you [must] believe in him and support him." [Allah] said, "Have you acknowledged and taken upon that My commitment?" They said, "We have acknowledged it." He said, "Then bear witness, and I am with you among the witnesses." (Surah 'Ahle-Imran, 81)

If you want wisdom, not one reached to his level ﷺ.

His wisdom was not that of the weak, but rather that of great determination.

His generosity is a gift that has a beginning but does not have an end! ﷺ.

Syedina Bilal ؓ, the trustee of the gifts of the ummah, was told by Him ﷺ, give it away, spend it Bilal; spend it Bilal!

Have you every heard anything like this before?

Have you every heard before Ahmad anything like this before ﷺ ?

Patience was tired from the patience of Muhammad ﷺ !

The patience of a very proud man, very pure.

He does not have any hate, and in his heart hate never finds residence ﷺ.

His jihad made his host tired, and through the course of his battles, his sword tired from his *jihad*! ﷺ.

In all His attributes, the closest to him was forgiveness ﷺ. Compared to anger, it was so much more close.

His was the forgiveness of the most strong.

He saw the weakness of his opponents, and gave them whatever they wanted! ﷺ.

Not only did he forgive, ﷺ, but he protected them from Omar ؓ, whose sword was always glinting out of its case, ready to destroy his enemies ﷺ.

Truth is a part of him, and it cannot be separated from him ﷺ.

The truth in him was clear, such that even his enemies confirmed and testified to this ﷺ.

His love for everyone, even those who are far away, was such that everyone thought he was the only one in His heart ﷺ.

Piety was that which did not allow him to sleep ﷺ.

Those long night nights of *munajaat* (conversation).

He would cry for us, missed us, and longed for us.

May my soul be a ransom for You ﷺ.

You are the Beloved of Allah ﷻ.

People blame me for only speaking about Muhammad, they say my only subject is You, and all that I mention is You ﷺ.

My response is Yes! My love is Muhammad! I worship Allah ﷻ by loving Muhammad! ﷺ.

My love is for the one who is my guidance, he is my owner, he is the one who freed me from the shackles of hellfire; the hellfire of *shyrk*, the hellfire of doubt, the hellfire of *dunya*! ﷺ.

He is my intercession on that very long Day.

My only joy, in this *dunya*, is the blessing of opening of my heart to this love and in *al akhira*, to be in His company ﷺ.

My only pride is to be from the ummah whose Prophet is Muhammad ﷺ!

Ar Rahman has never created anything like him ﷺ.

He is the only perfection! ﷺ.

Glory to the One who made him the Nur and the Guidance ﷺ.

Oh Allah ﷻ, we beseech you to send *salat* (prayers) upon him that never ends.

Allahuma salli alaa Syedina Muhammad wa alaa Ahli Syedina Muhammad

In a hadith, a bedoiun came to Rasulullah ﷺ and asked for rain. Rasulullah ﷺ said: "If Abu Talib was to be alive, he would have been happy to see this. Who will recite to us what he said?" Ali ؓ stood up and said: "Oh Rasulullah ﷺ, are you referring to his (Abu Talib) saying:

وأبيضُ يستسقي الغمــــــــام بوجهه ۞
ثـــــــــــــــــالِ اليتامى عصــــمةٍ للأرامل

Wa abyadu yus-stasqa al ghamama bi wajhi-hi thamali al yatama 'ismateen lil aramalee

That fair complexioned one, (referring to Rasulullah ﷺ) by whose face the prayer for rain is sought, He is the caretaker of orphans, and is the guardian of widows;

يلوذُ به الهلاك مــــــــــــن آل هاشمٍ ۞
فهم عنده في رحــــــــــمةٍ وفواضل

Yaluthu behe al hulaku min aaloo hashimen fahum endahu fi rahmatin wa fawadawlee

The family of Bani Hashim will seek refuge in him, and, under Him, they are in Mercy and Great Virtue.

لعمري لقد كلفِّــــــــــتُ وجداً بأحمد ۞
وإخوته دأب المحـــــــــبِّ المواصــــــل

La amree laqad kuliftu wajdan bi Ahmadi wa ikhwatihi da'bu al muhibi al muwwasili

[I swear], by my life, I have been occupied by the love of Ahmad and his brothers (his children); an occupation of continuous love.

فمن مثلُه في النـــــــــاس أي مؤمَّل ۞
إذا قاســـــــــــــــام الحكَّــــــــام عند التفاضل

Fa man mithlahu fi annasi ayu mu ammalin itha qasahu al hukkamu inda at tafadhuli

Who is like him! If his virtues were compared and judged against those who people seek from;

حليمٌ رشيد عادل غـــــــير طائش * يوالي إلـــــــهاً ليــــــس عنه بغافل

Haleemun Rasheedun 'Adelun ghairu ta'eshe yu waali ilahan laysah anhu be ghafaleen

Wise, Guided, Just, and never the oppressor; he is guarded by a Lord who is never heedless of him!

كريمُ المساعي مـــــــاجدٌ وابن ماجد * له إرثُ مجدٍ ثابـــــــتٍ غير ناصـــــــل

Kareemun al masa'ee majidun wa ibnu majidin lahu irthu majdin thabitin ghayru naasili

Generous towards all! He is Glorious and descends from Glory, a firm inheritance in Glory that does not waver!

وأيَّده ربُّ العباد بنصــــــــره * وأظهر دينــــــاً حقـــــــه غير زائل

Wa ayadahu rabbu-l ibadi bi narihi wa ad-hara deen-an haqquhu ghairu za'ili

And the Lord of Creation has supported him with His victory, and he has manifested a religion that will never disappear,

لقد علموا أن ابننا لا مكـــــــذبٌ * لدينا ولا يعنـــــــى بقولِ الأباطل

laqad 'alimu anna ibna-nah la mukazzabu la dayna wa la yu'nah bi qawli al abatili

And they knew that our son is not considered a liar by us and he is not concerned by those who say otherwise,

فأصبح فينا أحمـــــــدُ في أرومةٍ * يقصر عنها ســـــــورةُ المتطاول

fa asbaha feena Ahmadun fi aroom-atin yaqsuru anha suratu al mutataweli

He became praised amongst our entire honored lineage; no matter who competes they will end up short!

حدبت بنفسي دونــــــه وحميته * ودافعت عــــــــنه بالذّرى والكلاكل

Hadabtu bi nafsi dunahu wa hamaytuhu wa dafatu anhu bith-thura wal kalakili

I have protected him with my life, defended him by my shield and by my people."

Fath ul Bari (v2, Pg 575) – ibn Hajr 🙏

New Year – Muharram 1, 1435

1 Muharram 1435 – 5 November 2013

Today is the first of Muharram, from the year 1435 of *Hijrah*. This day is very important, and if we did not know this day, we would not know the day of Eid, the beginning of Ramadan, or the timing of *Hajj*.

In a Hadith narrated by Abu Hurairah ﷺ, Rasulullah ﷺ said, the best fast after Ramadan, is in the month of Allah ﷻ, Muharram; and the best prayer after the obligatory prayer (*fard*) is the night prayer, *qiyam ul layl*. (Sahih Muslim: 1163)

Muharram is the month that Rasulullah ﷺ called the month of Allah ﷻ.

It is very important for us as Muslims to understand the concepts of time and the calendar.

Allah ﷻ mentioned the months of the calendar, and highlighted the four sacred months, one of them being Muharram:

"Indeed, the number of months with Allah is twelve [lunar] months in the register of Allah [from] the day He created the heavens and the earth; of these, four are sacred. That is the correct religion, so do not wrong yourselves during them. And fight against the disbelievers collectively as they fight against you collectively. And know that Allah is with the righteous [who fear Him]." (Surah At-Tawbah: 36)

The importance of time can be seen in all that we do; *salah* (prayer) has a specific time, Hajj has a specific time and Ramadan has a specific time.

We also remember this day because during the time of the Rasulullah ﷺ, there was no method of keeping track of time with a calendar. Even during the time of Hadhrat Abu Bakr ﷺ and Hadhrat Omar ﷺ, there was no calendar. Here we briefly remind ourselves, that the calendar year was started at the time of Hadhrat

Omar ﷺ, as during his time the Muslim ummah had expanded far and wide, and as such communication and timing became of critical importance. In deciding the start of the calendar, Hadhrat Omar ﷺ consulted with the Sahaba, who suggested that it should start from the birth or death of Rasulullah ﷺ. But it was the suggestion of Imam Ali ﷺ which was accepted; his suggestion was to start the calendar at the event of the *hijrah* from Makkah to Madinah al Munawarah, as it signifies the success of the delivering, spreading and acceptance of the message.

So from this we learn that the Sahaba put in a lot of effort for us, the future generations of Muslims, in putting together the calendar and other efforts they have made. As such, it is important for us to remember the Sahaba, remember Hadhrat Abu Bakr, Omar, Uthman and Ali ﷺ and most importantly, remember the event of the *hijrah* that defines our time, by which we measure everything; it is in the event of the *hijrah* that Rasulullah left everything for the sake of Allah ﷺ.

Just look at the life of Rasulullah ﷺ in Makkah before, he was called Sadiq al Amin! He was the most respected amongst all strata of society, and the Quraysh. He ﷺ was held in such high regard that the Quraysh asked him to put the black stone in its place in the Kaaba ﷺ.

For Allah's ﷺ sake, Rasulullah ﷺ gave up everything so that we could receive the message!

The companions left everything for the sake of Allah ﷺ and Rasulullah ﷺ, such that everything we have rests on their sacrifices.

We must remember the sacrifices:

Khadijah gave everything.

Abu Bakr gave all he had, and left everyone to be in Rasulullah's company on the *hijrah*.

Imam Ali sacrificed all.

And the people of Madinah, who received and welcomed Rasulullah with such fervor.

Remember them all for how they have sacrificed for this Ummah.

For us, the beginning of the year is a chance to renew our *iman*.

Rasulullah said regarding this, that there is a polish for everything that removes rust, and the polish for the heart is the remembrance of Allah. (*Al-Bukhari*)

And we remind our brothers and our sisters to fast the 10th of Muharram. The greatness of fasting this day is related to us by Rasulullah, who when the Jews of Madinah fasted the 10th to commemorate the day Musa achieved success, Rasulullah stated that he should be much more happy as he is much closer to Musa.

Abu Qatada relates that the Holy Prophet said that the fast on the 10th of Muharram atones for the sins of the preceding year. (*Sahih Muslim*)

As we honour this day, we honour every day that is honoured by and that is close to Rasulullah. In saying this, it is also a blessing that the 1st of Muharram this year falls on a Monday, which is the day that Rasulullah was born. And when asked why he fasts on Mondays, he answered that that was the day he was born.

The day of Ashura, is also the day that the love of Rasulullah , his grandson, Syedina Imam Hussain Shaheed ﷺ, was martyred by those awful and hateful people at Karbala. May Allah ﷻ gather us with him, and all the *Saliheen* and *Shuhudah*, under the shade of Rasulullah ﷺ.

In ending, we congratulate the Ummah on the new year, and inshAllah may it be a year of *khair* (blessings), *rahma* (mercy), forgiveness, prosperity and unity for the Ummah of Rasulullah ﷺ, and we ask Allah ﷻ to make us closer to Him.

To the Mercy of Allah ﷺ

11 Muharram 1435 – 16 November 2013

Bismillah, all Praise to Him ﷻ, and Peace and Blessings upon His Beloved, Muhammad ﷺ.

Allah ﷻ, Great and Glorious, afore-time said, 'We sent you as Our Own Mercy to all the Worlds.'

Allah ﷻ made you Master of all of Creation.

From that I knew what you meant when you said: "If I had to choose a friend it would be Abu Bakr ؓ, but I have taken Allah ﷻ as my friend".

Ya Rasulullah ﷺ, *I know I am not your only one; how can I be? But know, you are the only one for me!*

I know that the Prophets, each and every one, raise their sights unto you; the entire heaven scrambled for a glimpse whilst Jibreel ؑ, master to the Angels, confessed his limit and came to a halt.

Ya Rasulullah ﷺ, *I know I am not your only one; how can I be? But know, you are the only one for me!*

Ya Rasulullah ﷺ !

Oh Beloved of Allah!

Oh Master of Creation!

Oh Friend of Allah!

I cannot conceal that

You are the only one for me!

All that I may possess or hold dear, be it family, friends or other, it is all the same to me. My pleasure lies in your happiness, as you are the only one for me.

Remember that young girl of Khabbab ibn al Aref, when she appealed to you that there was no one to milk their animals; you responded with your all-encompassing mercy, that you would be the one to milk for them. The young girl, aware of what had transpired, requested you to come again whenever you thought of milk. How enviously I recall that girl!

Remember the young man Said al Khudri ﷺ who invited you to his humble home, and upon remembering your Companions hunger, you assumed your role as host and invited them to feast. How I wish that I could be that young man or those that were invited!

Remember Abdullah ibn Masud ﷺ! The one who was blessed to carry your shoes under his arm wherever you went. Even Musa ﷺ himself would have been subdued at the light of Abdullah! How I envy him.

Remember Muadh ﷺ, your emissary to Yemen! You accompanied him on his departure, sharing your secret. I wish that I was the dust under Muadh's foot!

Remember Bilal ﷺ! The one you had raised, even above the Kaa'ba. His self-exile in Shaam, in order not to be in Al Madina, in which he saw you at every turn, ended when you approached him in his dream, and he again visited Al Madina to call for your joy. Relish in the joy he rejoiced in during the last moments of waiting!

Remember Zaid ibn Haritha ﷺ. The one who answered to the name "The Loved One of Rasulullah ﷺ," and after him his son, Osama, "The Son of the Loved One of Rasulullah ﷺ." Has anyone ever been given such a high and immortal title?

And remember Anas ﷺ, the one who had the fortune of the title, "Servant of Rasulullah ﷺ!" What good fortune it is to be remembered as such!

Ya Rasulullah ﷺ, I know I am not your only one; how can I be? But know, you are the only one for me!

Giving

22 Muharram 1435 - 27 November 2013

In a Hadith, narrated by Abu Darda ﷺ, Rasulullah ﷺ mentioned that there are two angels that record and pray for people if they give for the sake of Allah ﷻ and they pray that whatever they give to be replaced by something even better, and for those who are stingy, to allow what they have saved for themselves to go to waste.

Allah ﷻ followed this statement of Rasulullah ﷺ by revealing the *ayahs* in Surah Al-Layal (4-7) in which He ﷻ says:

"Indeed, your efforts are diverse. As for he who gives and fears Allah ﷻ, And believes in the best, WE will ease him toward ease."

In this *ayah*, Allah ﷻ highlights that those who give for the sake of Allah ﷻ will be guided to the best by Him!

This *ayah* was in fact revealed about Syedina Abu Bakr as-Sadiq ﷺ. The father of Syedina Abu Bakr ﷺ, Abu Quhafa ﷺ, was concerned as a father for his son's material well-being, even though he was not Muslim at the time. Syedina Abu Bakr ﷺ was freeing slaves who were elderly but his father said that he should keep them as they would be helpful for him and his friend Rasulullah ﷺ. Syedina Abu Bakr ﷺ responded by saying he only frees them for the sake of Allah ﷻ, so he has nothing further to consider when deciding to free them!

May Allah ﷻ give us the ability to follow Rasulullah ﷺ in all that we do.

Do Not Lose Hope

23 Muharram 1435 - 28 November 2013

A message for my dear brothers and sisters: **Do not lose hope! The Mercy is greater than anyone can begin to imagine!**

As such, we have highlighted a few verses to reflect upon in order for us to realize the Mercy and Blessings Allah ﷻ sent with Rasulullah ﷺ.

"And if We willed, We could surely do away with that which We revealed to you" - Surah Al-Isra: 86

In order to remember something, do not look towards your memory faculty, as to whether it is good or bad. But instead know that you will remember what Allah ﷻ wants you to remember!

"And to Daud We gave Sulaiman. A blessed slave, indeed he was one repeatedly turning back [to Allah]." - (Surah Sad: 30)

How many of us look and aspire for receiving praise from those around us? Once in our life, instead of looking at others for praise, we should hope to be mentioned by Allah ﷻ, as a blessed slave!

Who sees you when you arise "And your movement among those who prostrate." - (Surah Ash-Shura: 219)

And at night, know that when you are in *sujud* (prostration), you are not alone! Allah ﷻ has grouped you with the best of His creation.

"And Nuh had certainly called Us, and [We are] the best of responders." (Surah As-Saffat: 75)

Always remember whom to call upon when you are in a dire situation. When problems and challenges arise, think about who we should call upon, instead of simply reaching out to those around us.

"So when the Qur'an is recited, then listen to it and keep quiet so that you may receive mercy." - (Surah Al-Araf: 204)

The Mercy of Allah ﷻ is so close to us that even if we were to remain quiet, we could still receive it!

"When you received it with your tongues and said with your mouths that of which you had no knowledge...." - (Surah An-Nur: 15)

In this *ayah* Allah ﷻ mentions the spreading of rumors, with regards to Syedina Aisha ؓ. In the time of *fitna* (tribulation), all of our organs remain still and paralyzed, except for the tongue. So in a time of fitna watch what you say!

"And do not confer favor to acquire more." - (Surah Al-Muddathir: 6)

Do not count things, especially your deeds. Imam Hasan ؓ said not to look at our deeds as something great or noteworthy, as we do not know whether they will be accepted or not!

"And the pains of childbirth drove her to the trunk of a palm tree. She said, 'Oh, I wish I had died before this and was in oblivion, forgotten.'" - (Surah Mariam: 23)

When Mariam ؑ became pregnant, she worried about people's reaction, so much so that she wish she had died before all of this. She did not know that she carried a *Nabi* in her womb! We do not know what *rahma* and *ni'mah* (mercy and blessings) lay behind the trials we face.

Do not worry about what has not been achieved, obtained or missed in this *dunya*. On Day of Standing, neither our money, family or friends will help us. The only one that will be sought is Rasulullah ﷺ!

May Allah ﷻ cover you with His Mercy, and gather us with Rasulullah ﷺ.

Munajaat

14 Safar 1435 – 18 December 2013

Oh Allah ﷻ, You see where I am and You listen to what I say; You know me Ya Rabbi and You know about my situation more than any of Your slaves.

Oh Allah ﷻ, my *shikwa* and complaint is only to You. Not to any of Your slaves. So Ya Rabbi, accept me with all my shortcomings.

Oh Allah ﷻ, I knocked Your door, so open the door of Your blessings, and protect me from the tests.

Oh Allah ﷻ, "You are the One who has the ability to help, and You made the strong to help the weak; You made jinn in the service of Sule*iman* ﷺ, birds in the company of Nabi Daud ﷺ and you made the fire easy on Syedina Ibrahim ﷺ".

Ya Rabbi, choose the best of Your slaves to be around me, those who are full of *khair* (blessings) and keep me in *khair*; and those who are not in *khair*, make them away from me me away from them.

Oh Allah ﷻ, make things easy for me, sustain me from a way that I have never thought of.

Oh Allah ﷻ, You help with Your Power and Ability, and with Your *Izzat* (high esteem), You are the most Able, You alone.

Oh Allah ﷻ, I ask You in awe of Your Greatness, with the hope of Your *Rahma* (mercy) to bless with *khair* my *deen*, *dunya*, life and future. And to bless me in *dunya* before *akhira*.

Oh Allah ﷻ, I come to You on the lack of my ability and weakness, and believe I am nothing.

Oh Allah ﷻ, I beg You, Ya Rabbi, to remove all thoughts and issues.

Oh Allah ﷻ, prefer me, and make none over me.

Oh Allah ﷻ, support me, and none over me.

Oh Allah ﷻ, help me in my weakness to over come my weakness, and grant me success, success against all fears. Shower me with *rizq* (sustenance) from Your imagination, success from You with no limit, and *khair* from You that is not counted.

Oh Allah ﷻ, if my *rizq* is in the heavens, send it down, and if it is lies in he earth, then take it out; if it is far, bring it close, and if it is close make it easy; if little than make it a lot, and if a lot put *baraka* (blessing) in it; and the same for those I love, and those who love me.

Oh Allah ﷻ, grant peace of mind to everyone who is going through a difficult moment, everyone wiping their eyes from pain. Grant them all happiness in their hearts, and grant them tranquillity, and make their hope in You.

Oh Allah ﷻ, forgive me, my parents, teachers and those I love and those who love me. Make us from the people of *Jannah* with Your Great *Rahma*.

Oh Allah ﷻ, everyone who has a favour on us, grant them ease in *dunya* and *akhira*.

Oh Allah ﷻ, may we be blessed to see You and Rasulullah ﷺ. Blessed to have a good ending. Blessed in our *dunya* and *akhira*.

Oh Allah ﷻ, by the number of Your creation that we know and do not know, from the beginning of creation to the end, we ask You to send Your blessings upon our *ruh*, our heart, our mind our love, Rasulullah ﷺ, his pure family and blessed companions.

Bismillah-ir Rahman-ir Raheem
"O Prophet, indeed We have sent you as a witness and a bringer of good tidings and a warner. And one who invites to Allah, by His permission, and an illuminating lamp."
(Surah Al-Ahzab: 45-46)

Rasulullah

The Source of all Change Towards Khair

19 Safar 1435 - 23 December 2013

Allah ﷻ wants all the *khair* (blessing) for us because He is the source of all *khair*.

In Surah An-Nisa, Allah ﷻ speaks about human nature, and the fact that mankind was created with weakness. Abdullah ibn Abbas ﵂, commenting on this, said that this weakness is not only a physical weakness, but rather it is a weakness in facing our desires.

The One who created us and our desires Knows what we are like, and when He tells us or identifies in us things we should avoid, He has in fact made it easier for us to overcome those obstacles, in this case our desires. Among the things that will help us in this fight is to trust Allah ﷻ.

In Surah Al Baqarah (158), Allah ﷻ mentions that He wants to make things easy for you, and He wants you to see His Greatness, His Guidance and to be grateful to Him.

It is human nature to love wealth and *dunya* and all that is connected to them; and in that regard, people are very weak in facing and surmounting their desires.

Allah ﷻ says in Surah Al-Fajr (20) and Surah Al-Adiyat (8) that the love of wealth is an intense desire.

Now the *fitna* (tribulation) and desire of money, and the challenge of facting that desire, affects the best and wisest of people.

Hakeem ibn Huzaim ibn Khuwalyd ﵂ was known to be a wise man among the Quraysh, and a sign of this was the fact that he was born inside the Kaaba, which the Quraysh took as a sign of his wisdom, as they revered the Kaaba and only allowed nobility to enter it.

His mother and father were allowed in, and during their visit, he was born.

Hakeem ﷺ was not from among the early believers, even with all his wisdom, and in fact, he became *Muslim* very late. He also had the honor of being the nephew of Syeda Khadijah al Kubra ﷺ.

When Hakeem ﷺ became a *Muslim*, he travelled to Madinah, and upon arrival saw a completely different society; one in which the Ansar loved and cared and only wanted to be with Rasulullah ﷺ. The Ansar even used to stay hungry in order to give to others who did not have means, as the Ansar loved to give.

Allah ﷻ described them in the Quran in Surah Al-Hashr (9), when He said they prefer to give things even if they are in absolute need of them.

Once Rasulullah ﷺ asked the gathering who will host his guests, a man from the Ansar stood up. He went home to his wife and realizing that the only thing they had was their children's food, he told her to put the children to bed and turn off the lights, so that they can give the food to the guests and no one would know of their situation!

Hakeem ﷺ was fond of money, and he had a weakness in facing his desires even after accepting Islam. This shows us that everyone has his own weakness and desires, as well as their own level and ability.

In an authentic Hadith in Sahih al-Bukhari (1403) it is narrated that when Hakeem ﷺ came to Madinah, he asked Rasulullah ﷺ for money on numerous occasions, and Rasulullah ﷺ fulfilled his request each time.

However, after a certain number of times (in some narrations three, in others left open), Rasulullah ﷺ said, "*Ya Hakeem! Verily this money is sweet and green...*"

And here we must take a moment to say how lucky Hakeem ؓ was to be called by his name by the Master of Creation ﷺ!

In addition, if we look at the exact words Rasulullah ﷺ used to describe this situation, we notice that money is a masculine word, but the words "sweet" and "green" are feminine. If we compared this to the word "*dunya*", we realize this is also a feminine word, and that by using these words, Rasulullah ﷺ was describing all the desires that we may face.

We should also note that the adjectives used were sensory, and allude to physical, visual and tasting of this particular desire. By using such adjectives, Rasulullah ﷺ is also saying here that you are not alone, everyone faces desires like you.

The Hadith continues: "*Whoever receives money and has a generous heart, Allah ﷻ will put khair in what he receives. However, whoever takes with greed will never have any khair in what they take...*"

In this Hadith, we see that in everything that you take, it is not about what you are taking, it is about you! It is a reflection of you! If you are generous, it will never matter how much you have as you will have *baraka*; but if you are corrupt and greedy, no matter how much you have it will never be enough.

The Hadith continues: "*For the one whose heart has greed, he will keep eating but will never be full...*"

It is all about the person and their heart, with regards to any desire, whether it be money, food, or any other desire.

"*the upper hand is better than the lower...*" as it is better to give than to take.

In explanation of this, there are five different "hands" we can assume:

1) Hand that gives only – upper hand (the best)

2) Hand that takes only – lower hand

3) Hand that takes without asking

4) Hand that takes by asking

5) Hands that asks without any need for what they are asking (the worst)

Hakeem ؓ was older than Rasulullah ﷺ by thirteen years, but look at how difficult it is to change. Here we must highlight the approach and the patience of Rasulullah ﷺ that took Hakeem ؓ on this journey, and also the patience of Rasulullah ﷺ to allow him to ask him for money on so many occasions before deciding it is ready to take him on this journey!

Hakeem ؓ then said, "*I swear by the One who has sent you with the absolute truth, I will never ask anyone after you until I die.*" Hakeem ؓ had now understood.

The wisest man, whether in *jalahiya* (ignorance) or in *iman* (belief) keeps his promise. And wise men only befriend those who keep their promises.

Allah ﷻ mentioned in Surah Al-Baqarah (177) and Surah Ar-Ra'd (20) those who keep their promise, which highlights the importance of keeping promises in this *deen*; and the *munafiqeen* (hypocrites) are the ones who do not keep their promises.

Hakeem ؓ, from that day, kept his promise and never asked anyone for anything till his death. In fact, Hakeem ؓ went even further: he refused to take anything given to him either!

The Hadith continues to tell us about the long life of Hakeem ؓ, in which Syedina Abu Bakr ؓ attempted to give him a share of the bounty the Muslims had received, which Hakeem ﷺ refused. Hadhrat Omar ﷺ tried to give him a share of the bounty, but Hakeem ﷺ refused. Syedina Omar ﷺ, being a person known for his justice, at the response of Hakeem ﷺ rose on the pulpit and proclaimed "Oh Muslims, know that I gave him his rights and he chose not to take it."

The same occurred during the time of Hadhrat Uthman ﷺ, Syedina Ali ﷺ, and even after that! Hakeem ﷺ was granted a very long life, which was a test of his *iman* and steadfastness in his promise.

When his time came, Hakeem ﷺ died with a lot of *khair*, which points to the beginning of the Hadith.

We should reflect on this journey, where he started out and where he ended up; an ending of *khair* and *baraka*.

Also, we should reflect upon the *sabr* of Rasulullah ﷺ!

And because Hakeem ﷺ was blessed, he became in a position to change his attitude and situation.

May Allah ﷻ make us from the people of *khair*, and to hold strong to our promise while facing all trials and tribulations (*fitna*).

Also, as we have seen in the example of Hakeem ﷺ, great people go for perfection, and in any given moment, it is never too late to change, as long as we have hope in Allah ﷻ and Rasulullah ﷺ.

Allahumma salli alaa Syedina Muhammad wa alaa Ahli Syedina Muhammad

Question: How do I know if My *Iman* is increasing?

22 Safar 1435 - 26 December 2013

Instead of speaking about the signs of *iman* increasing, it is better to speak about how one can increase their *iman*, as there is no limit to how much *iman* can increase. Rasulullah ﷺ said in a Hadith *"Having a good thought of Allah ﷻ is, in itself, the best form of ibadah,"* (Imam al-Hakim) and Rasulullah ﷺ mentioned that we should "renew our *iman*." (Imam Ahmad).

Iman is like a tree, if you water it with a good source and care for it, the tree bears fruit; however, if you do not water it, or water it with a corrupted source and do not care for it, the tree will be fruitless.

With regards to increasing *iman*, there are a few points to mention:

When reading the Qur'an, we should read it with contemplation. In Surah At-Tawbah (124), Allah ﷻ says *"When a surah is revealed, some people will say 'Whose iman has increased by reading this part,' and for those who believe it will increase them in iman and happiness."* When reading the Qur'an, the best way to read is to stop in every *ayah*, and to contemplate its meaning. If the *ayah* is about *jannah*, we should ask for it; if the *ayah* mentions a command from Allah ﷻ, we should ensure that we are doing it; if the *ayah* prevents us from something, we should ask ourselves if we have refrained from it; if the *ayah* asks us to make *tasbih*, to check that we are making *tasbih*; if the *ayah* commands us to make *salawat*, to reflect on how much *salawat* we make; if the *ayah* describes the universe and the creation of Allah ﷻ, to reflect and to think about the Greatness of Allah ﷻ.

In order to increase *iman* we should seek Allah's ﷻ help. In Surah Baqara (186) Allah ﷻ says *"Ask me and I will respond to you, and if my servants ask you about Me, tell them I am very close."* Allah ﷻ loves *dua*, and Rasulullah ﷺ said *"dua is ibadah itself"* (narrated in an authentic Hadith by Nu'man ibn Bashir ﷺ). *"Allah ﷻ*

is the most shy when His servants ask Him." When we make *dua* to Allah ﷻ it shows our humility, dependency, *ibadah* of the heart and focuses everything on Allah ﷻ by giving up from asking everyone else. Inherent in *dua* is also the fear of whether or not the *dua* will be accepted, full reliance on Allah ﷻ, glorification of His Greatness, *dhikr*, choosing Him over others, seeking Him over others and shows our love towards Him, *"as you would never ask one you did not love."* Also, even when we physically raise our hands in *dua*, it shows that we are begging Allah ﷻ and are fully reliant on Him.

In addition, *iman* is increased by sending *salawat* and loving Rasulullah ﷺ. As we know from the Hadith that no one's *iman* can be complete unless they love Rasulullah ﷺ more than their money, their children and all of creation. Not only does *iman* increase with this love, but this love is *iman* itself! There are three things that if achieved, are also related to increasing *iman*: 1) to love Allah ﷻ and Rasulullah ﷺ more than love for anything (including *jannah*), 2) to love your brother and sister for the sake of Allah ﷻ, and 3) To hate your past bad deeds as you hate the fire of *jahannum*.

Also, what increases *iman* is *dhikr*-Allah, the example of which is those who remember versus those who do not are similar to those who are alive and those who are dead. The real life is *iman*. As Allah ﷻ mentions in Surah Ar-Ra'd (28) *"Verily, only by the remembrance of Allah ﷻ do hearts achieve peace and tranquillity."* And in Surah Al-Anfal (2) Allah ﷻ says *"Verily the believers are those who when Allah ﷻ is mentioned their hearts become fearful, and when the verses are recited to them their iman increases, and they rely on Allah ﷻ fully."* And in Surah Muhammad (17) Allah ﷻ says *"And those who are guided, Allah ﷻ will increase them in guidance and He will grant them taqwa (awareness of Allah ﷻ/piety)."*

That which also increases *iman* is to love to be in the company of the righteous ones; either to be with them or to love to be with them. Allah ﷻ says in Surah At-Tawbah (119) *"Oh you who believe, be aware of Allah ﷻ and be in the company of the righteous ones."* Look at them, be with them, this is *ibadah*. Going into their company and believing they are the best company and better than you, is *ibadah* and increases *iman*. Syedina Omar ﷺ said to the companions "let us come together and increase our *iman*." Hadhrat Muadh ﷺ said "let us sit together and be *mu'mins* for an hour."

Also in increasing our *iman*, we should give importance to completing our *fard* (obligatory) actions on time and to carry out the sunnah, as "the most loved forms of *ibadah* to Allah ﷻ are the continuous forms of *ibadah*, even if they are small."

Another way to increase *iman* is through *tafakkur*, or reflection and contemplation. *Tafakkur* shows us the Greatness of Allah ﷻ, and additionally, we should try to avoid people who speak of inconsequential things. Hadhrat Omar ﷺ said if it were not for two things, I would not want to be alive: the first, *salah*, and the second to be in the company of people who choose their words as people choose the best of food. Also, in this *dunya*, we dwell on instruction manuals for things that we do, but if we were to look and reflect on our body and composition, we would see Allah ﷻ and His Greatness.

We should also use our time wisely and try to always be in a state of *dhikr*, as Allah ﷻ says in Surah Ahle-Imran (191) *"Make dhikr, while standing, walking or laying, and keep thinking about the creation of Allah ﷻ, whose contemplation will lead you to realize that all this was created for a purpose which will lead you to one reality."* After this *ayah*, there is no excuse for free time!

Also from the things that increase *iman*, is to visit the graveyard as it reminds us of the *akhira*. As Rasulullah ﷺ mentioned that hearts become rusted like metal, the companions asked Rasulullah ﷺ how their hearts can be cleansed of this rust, to which he ﷺ responded that to remember death and to read the Qur'an. Also, to make *tawbah* is from the acts that increase *iman*. In addition, to be in a state of *rida*, complete satisfaction, with Allah ﷻ. Those in the state of rida know that whatever situation they are in or that which is around them is the best and has been placed in front of them from Allah ﷻ who wants the best for them.

When you go through tests, know that these tests are from Allah ﷻ, and to face them with patience increases your *iman*. In Surah Ahle-Imran (173) Allah ﷻ says speaking about the believers *"people will come to them and tell them that all are against them and that they should move away in fear, the believers will instead not respond in fear, but rather this will increase their iman! And their response will be 'Sufficient for us is Allah ﷻ, and He is the best Sponsor."* For the believers, regardless of the test, nothing will happen to them. Yes, maybe their physical bodies may be affected, but their heart and soul is not harmed and does not waver in the face of any test, but rather it is strengthened with *iman*!

Lastly, the best thing we can implement to increase our *iman* is to have the best of characters, as the best *iman* is of those who have the best of characters, and as we know, Allah ﷻ praised Rasulullah ﷺ for having the best of characters in the Qur'an.

May Allah ﷻ guide us and strengthen our *iman*.

Allahumma salli alaa Syedina Muhammad wa alaa Ahli Syedina Muhammad.

Bismillah-ir Rahman-ir Raheem
"Allah is the Light of the heavens and the earth."
(Surah An-Nur: 35)

Surah An-Nur:
How to Deal and have Adab with the Nur

25 Safar 1435 - 29 December 2013

Allah ﷻ is Nur, and He sent Rasulullah ﷺ as a Nur from Him ﷻ. As such, Allah ﷻ did not send us His Habib and Nur ﷺ without giving us guidance on how to deal with him ﷺ. Allah ﷻ mentions in the last three *ayahs* of Surah An-Nur (62-64):

The believers are only those who believe in Allah and His Messenger and, when they are [meeting] with him for a matter of common interest, do not depart until they have asked his permission. Indeed, those who ask your permission, [O Muhammad] - those are the ones who believe in Allah and His Messenger. So when they ask your permission for something of their affairs, then give permission to whom you will among them and ask forgiveness for them of Allah . Indeed, Allah is Forgiving and Merciful.

Do not make [your] calling of the Messenger among yourselves as the call of one of you to another. Already Allah knows those of you who slip away, concealed by others. So let those beware who dissent from the Prophet's order, lest fitnah strike them or a painful punishment.

Unquestionably, to Allah belongs whatever is in the heavens and earth. Already He knows that upon which you [stand] and [knows] the Day when they will be returned to Him and He will inform them of what they have done. And Allah is Knowing of all things.

Allah ﷻ in these verses makes clear that the believers are not only those that just believe in Allah ﷻ and Rasulullah ﷺ, but they are those that seek permission from Rasulullah ﷺ, and that he ﷺ is the one who asks Allah ﷻ for forgiveness on the behalf of the believers. Allah ﷻ here is showing us how to have adab with Rasulullah ﷺ, and He continues to say that Rasulullah ﷺ has the discretion as to who he will grant permission and forgiveness to.

Allah ﷻ continues to describe how to deal with His Nur and Beloved ﷺ by saying that we should not call him like we call others, otherwise a grave punishment may befall us ﷺ. Look at the love of Allah ﷻ for Rasulullah ﷺ!

This is our gift to you on this auspicious day. Read these *ayahs*, think about them, reflect upon them, and see how you can implement them, as verily there is no *iman* without loving and respecting Rasulullah ﷺ more than anyone.

Hikmah: Ni'mah from Allah ﷻ

27 Safar 1435 - 31 December 2013

Do not be deceived by appearances

And *ni'mah* you see bestowed upon others

How many *ni'mahs* you may see as a blessing

When actually, it may be a burden for the person

Be pleased with what Allah ﷻ has given you

Trust Allah's ﷻ choice for you

It might be that you carry tons of blessings, *khair* and treasures

That Allah ﷻ has bestowed upon you

Allah ﷻ is All Knowing, All Wise and the Best Judge

Allah ﷻ said in the Qur'an:

If you try to count the ni'mah of Allah ﷻ, you will never be able to do so…"
(Surah An-Nahl: 18)

If Allah ﷻ was to ask us to give thanks for every *ni'mah* that He has given us, that would be the worst of punishments!

Allah ﷻ mentions that He is the "All Forgiving and All Merciful" at the end of the *ayah*, as He ﷻ knows in advance that we cannot give thanks for all the ni'mah He has granted us!

May Allah ﷻ grant you and I contentment in the Allah's ﷻ decree, and may He grant us the company of Rasulullah ﷺ.

Allahumma salli alaa Syedina Muhammad wa alaa Ahli Syedina Muhammad

Rabi ul Awwal Mubarak

1 Rabi ul Awwal 1435 - 2 January 2014

The month of Rabi-ul Awwal has begun, and for that, we send you congratulations.

These moments are ones of happiness and joy, as Allah ﷻ mentions in the Quran:

"Say 'be joyous in what Allah ﷻ sent in His Blessings and Mercy, as that should cause greater happiness than anything else." (Surah Yunus: 58)

Here Allah ﷻ is giving us two great reasons to be happy: His Blessings and Mercy.

Allah ﷻ mentions the gift of His Blessings in Surah An-Nisa (113), when He says speaking to Rasulullah ﷺ, *"Allah ﷻ blessing upon you is so great."*

With regards to the gift of Mercy, Allah ﷻ says in Surah Al-Anbiya (107) *"We have not sent you other than to be a Mercy to all the worlds,"* referring to Rasulullah ﷺ.

And from this *ayah*, it is clear for the believers that the source of both Blessings and Mercy is Rasulullah ﷺ, as he is a Blessing sent by Allah ﷻ to be a Mercy to all the worlds! ﷺ.

Rabi-ul Awwal is the month of the birth of Rasulullah ﷺ and as such it is for us the Mercy of Allah ﷻ, the Blessing of Allah ﷻ and the Nur of Allah ﷻ.

We congratulate everyone at this auspicious moment, and urge everyone to enjoy these moments. May Allah ﷻ unite us with Rasulullah ﷺ.

Allahumma salli alaa Syedina Muhammad wa alaa Ahli Syedina Muhammad. Allahumma barak alaa Syedina Muhammad wa alaa Ahli Syedina Muhammad.

Rasulullah's ﷺ uncle Al Abbas ؓ said to him: "O Messenger of Allah, I wish to praise you." Rasulullah ﷺ replied: "Go ahead - may Allah ﷻ adorn your mouth with silver!" He said:

من قبلها طبت في الظلال وفي مستودع حيث يخصف الورق

min qabliha tibta fi addilali wa fi mustaw-da'en haithu yu-khsafu al waraqu

*Before you came to this world
you were blessed in the shadows and in the repository (i.e. loins)
in the time when they (Adam and Eve) covered themselves with leaves.*

ثم هبطت البلاد لا بشر انت ولامضغة ولا علق

thumah habbat-al biladah la basharun anta wa la muzqatun wa la alaqu

*Then you descended to the earth,
neither as a human being, nor as a piece of flesh, nor as a clot.*

بل نطفة تركب السفين وقد ألجم نسرا واهله الغرق

Bil nutfatun tarkabu as-safeena wa qad uljima nisrun wa ahlahu al gharaqu

*But as a drop that boarded the ark
when the flood destroyed the eagle and the rest of the idols:*

تنقل من صالب الى رحم اذا مضى عالم بدا طبق

Tu-naqalu min sulbin illah raheemin itha madah alamun bada tabaqu

*A drop that progressed from the loins to the wombs
in the succession of the worlds and the heavens*

حتى احتوى بيتك المهيمن من خندف علياء تحتها النطق

Hattah ihtawa baytu-ka al muhayminu min khandafin aliya'a tah-ta-ha an-natqu

Until the Preserver of All made your immense honor issue in the highest summit of the line of Khindif.

وانت لما ولدت اشرقت الأرض وضاءت بنورك الافق

Wa anta lamma wu-litta ashraqat al ardhu wada'at bi nur-rika al ufuwqu

And then, when you were born, a light rose over the earth until it illuminated the horizon with its radiance.

فنحن في ذلك الضياء وفي النور وسبل الرشاد نخترق

Fa-nahnu fi tha-lika ad-dhiya'e wa fi an-nuri wa subuli ar-rashadi nakh-tariqu

*We are in that illumination
and that original light and those paths of guidance -- and thanks to them pierce through.*

Tawfiq is from Him ﷻ

6 Rabi ul Awwal 1435 - 7 January 2014

Allah ﷻ said in the Qur'an, in Surah Al-Baqarah (185), that He wanted to make things easy for you, not difficult. In saying this, Allah ﷻ is telling you that He wants you for Himself, and that He ﷻ, only wants *khair* for His creation.

In the aforementioned *ayah*, even when commanding you to fast, stopping and restraining from things you normally enjoy, He commands you to this because He wants the best for you! ﷻ.

In this life, whenever you see Allah ﷻ giving you *tawfiq* to be in the company of the people of Allah ﷻ, people who encourage you to do good things and become closer to Allah ﷻ and Rasulullah ﷺ, be sure Allah ﷻ wanted *khair* for you!

And when you see Allah ﷻ give *tawfiq* to you to ask, beg, and make *dua* for anything whether it be minor or major, big or small, *khair* or protection from evil, be sure the He would not give you the *tawfiq* to make *dua* unless He wanted to give to you your request. He made you ask! ﷻ.

When you see Allah ﷻ give you the *tawfiq* to make *dhikr*, the *tawfiq* to increase the amount of *dhikr*, to think about Him, to do things for His creation, to become close to His people, and to busy yourself in tasks for His sake, be sure that Allah ﷻ loves you! And for those whom He loves He will grant them success, support them and respond to everything they say ﷻ.

Finally take this example – Imam Hasan al Basri ﷺ, the great *wali*, *tab'ee* and scholar, taught us something very important, and this is our gift for those we love:

Once Imam Hasan al Basri ﷺ was seen all night making *dua*. What do you think he was making *dua* for? What was he asking and saying? Why was he raising his hands all night?

The *dua* he was making was for Allah ﷻ to forgive those who oppressed him! *SubhanAllah!*

A man who saw Imam Hasan ؓ said "Ya Aba Saeed, you make so much *dua* for those who oppressed you that I wish to be one of them! Why do you make such a *dua*?"

Imam Hasan al Basri ؓ responded by saying, "*Do not you see what Allah ﷻ says,'…those who forgive and reconcile such that the situation is better than it was before, their reward is guaranteed by Allah ﷻ…!*" (Surah Ash-Shura: 40)

This is our *deen*!

This is the *Ruh* Muhammadiyya ﷺ!

These are the things that should make us proud.

May Allah ﷻ give us the *tawfiq* for every *khair*, beneficial knowledge and good deed.

Allahumma salli alaa Syedina Muhammad wa alaa Ahli Syedina Muhammad

Hajj and Umrah

10 Rabi ul Awwal 1435 - 11 January 2014

Allah ﷻ said in the Qur'an in Surah Al-Baqarah: Complete *Hajj* and *Umrah* for the sake of Allah ﷻ.

In a Hadith narrated by Imam Bukhari ﷫, Abu Hurraira ﷺ said that Rasulullah ﷺ said that between one *Umrah* and another *Umrah*, Allah ﷻ forgives all sins between them. In another Hadith it is mentioned that those who go to *Hajj* and *Umrah* are the guests of Allah ﷻ, and Allah ﷻ made it compulsory upon Himself to honor His guests.

So going to *Umrah*, is accepting the invitation of Allah ﷻ, leaving your family for sake of Allah ﷻ, taking a break for the sake of Allah ﷻ, as if you leaving everything behind you and facing Allah ﷻ alone.

Going on the journey of *Umrah* is one of the best things you can do, and there is a lot of *baraka* you gain in *dunya* and in *al akhira*. In a Hadith narrated by Imam Tirmidhi ﷫, Rasulullah ﷺ said to keep doing *Hajj* and *Umrah*, as it removes poverty by gaining the forgiveness of Allah ﷻ; and Rasulullah ﷺ completed four *Umrahs* during his life.

In the journey of *Umrah*, every act you do brings you closer to Allah ﷻ; and even for your intention you get a reward, for every *salah* in the *Haram Sharif* you receive the reward of 100,000 *salah*, and for every step of *tawaf* you receive a reward. In a Hadith narrated by Abdullah ibn Omar ﷺ, Rasulullah ﷺ said in every step of *tawaf* you receive a reward and a sin is removed, as narrated by Imams Ahmad, Tirmidhi, Hakim and ibn Khuzayma ﷫.

Also the money you spend in your *Umrah* is money spent for the best reason, and it has been spent in the best way. When Syeda Ayesha ﷺ was going for *Umrah*, Rasulullah ﷺ said to her, you will get the reward according to what you spend and according to your effort, as narrated by Imam

Hakim ﷺ. Going to the very places of *Umrah*, is going back to where Ibrahim ﷺ went, going back to the Ka'ba which they built, going to Safa and Marwa in the footsteps of Syeda Hajr ﷺ, and everywhere you go there, you are following the footsteps of Rasulullah ﷺ!

Allah ﷻ says in Surah Ahle-Imran "*Say, 'If you really love Allah ﷻ follow me, and Allah ﷻ will love you.*" What better way to show this love, than to follow the footsteps of Rasulullah ﷺ in *tawaf*, *saiy* between Safa and Marwa, and going to his *masjid* which was built by his blessed hands ﷺ!

One thing we will say to all our brothers and sisters, in your journey you need to prepare yourself with a righteous intention, by asking forgiveness, by making a lot of *tauba* from now, and by making a lot of *dua* that Allah ﷻ accepts this journey from you.

Also, there is a great benefit of saying the *talbiyah*, and it is narrated that every Muslim who makes *talbiyah*, all the creation around him, including trees and stones, will repeat the *talbiyah* with him!

Those who do *Hajj* and *Umrah* are the guests of Allah ﷻ. Allah invited them, and Allah ﷻ has already accepted them.

May Allah ﷻ bless your journey.

Astaghfar - Forgiveness

10 Rabi ul Awwal 1435 - 11 January 2014

Allah ﷻ said in Surah Nuh, telling us about Prophet Nuh's ﷺ advice to his people: "*I said to them ask forgiveness form your Lord, verily He is All Forgiving, and when you ask for forgiveness He will bless with rain and a lot of blessings.*"

Rasulullah ﷺ said in a Hadith "*Oh people, ask Allah's ﷻ forgiveness, verily I ask seventy times a day,*" and in some narrations one-hundred times a day.

Why did Rasulullah ﷺ ask for forgiveness even though he does not commit sins, and Allah ﷻ said in the beginning of Surah Al-Fath, Allah ﷻ has forgiven your past and whatever is in the future. Why? Because Allah ﷻ said in the Qur'an "*Verily Allah ﷻ loves those who ask for forgiveness.*"

So our advice for those we love is do not plan a lot, but instead, ask Allah ﷻ to forgive you a lot; verily, Allah ﷻ opens with *astaghfar*, doors that cannot be opened with planning. So let us say:

Astaghfirullah

I seek forgiveness of Allah ﷻ.

Astaghfirullah al-'Adheem

I seek forgiveness of Allah ﷻ the Most Great.

Astaghfirullah al-'Adheem wa atubu ilaih

I seek forgiveness of Allah ﷻ the Most Great and I repent unto Him.

Astaghfirullah al-'Adheemal-ladhi la ilaha illa Huwal-Hayyul-Qayyum wa atubu ilaih

I seek the forgiveness of Allah the Most Great, Whom there is none worthy except Him, the Living, The Eternal, and I repent unto Him ﷻ.

In a Hadith narrated by Imam Tirmidhi ﷺ, anyone who makes the above *astaghfar*, Allah ﷻ forgives him or her from even the major sins.

Allahumma Ya Ghiyathi Al Mustaghitheen bi Haqq, la illaha illallah anta subahanika inni kuntum minathaulimeen, salli alaa Syedina Muhammad wa alaa Ahli Syedina Muhammad.

May Allah bless you with every *khair*.

Best of Characters – Khuluqul Adheem

25 Rabi ul Awwal 1435 - 26 January 2014

Bismillah-ir Rahman-ir Raheem.

Allah ﷻ said in Surah Al-Qalam (4) speaking about Rasulullah ﷺ: *"Verily, you have exalted the best of characters."*

Allah ﷻ here uses the word "Adheem" (Greatest) speaking about the character of Rasulullah ﷺ.

In choosing the word "Adheem" it shows that everything about Rasulullah ﷺ is great, and after the witness of this by Allah ﷻ, there is no need for any other witness, as Allah ﷻ says at the end of Surah Al-Fath (28): *"He is the One who sent the Messenger with guidance and the religion of absolute truth and made it over all religion, and Allah ﷻ is sufficient as a Witness."*

And yet Allah ﷻ showed us that this greatness of Rasulullah ﷺ was witnessed by his enemies and companions alike, and no one in history has had such witnesses!

The witnesses were men, women, children, leaders, companions, and his wives; all these witnesses mentioned nothing other than the greatness of Rasulullah ﷺ. Even from among his enemies, no one attacked his character ﷺ.

Imagine this: during *Hajj al-Widah*, over one-hundred thousand people gathered in front of Rasulullah ﷺ from the Sahaba, including children, slaves, men, women, and those inside his household and those outside his household, did not speak about anything regarding Rasulullah ﷺ other than the greatness of Rasulullah ﷺ. No one in history has had every aspect of their lives recorded in such detail, as we have the recorded details of Rasulullah ﷺ. We know how Rasulullah ﷺ washed, his clothing, and every imaginably possible act. All of this attempts to exemplify his greatness ﷺ!

Hafiz Shamsuddin Sakhawi ﷺ, the 9th century Imam, wrote a book speaking about history and its importance, and blaming those who do not study history. Imam Sakhawi ﷺ mentioned that if we were only to write the names of the books that were written regarding Rasulullah ﷺ, it would fill twenty volumes! This was over five-hundred years ago, and does not include the books that were destroyed during the Mongol invasion.

By studying the *seerah* of Rasulullah ﷺ, we are seeking guidance and the Nur. In Surah Al-Maidah (15) Allah ﷻ says that he sent us a *"Nur from Him and a Clear Book."*

Syeda Aisha ﷺ mentioned that Rasulullah's ﷺ character was the Quran. From this we can take a few lessons. Firstly, this statement is coming from the wife of Rasulullah ﷺ and although we may be able to act a certain way in front of others, our true selves come out in our homes, which shows the weight of this statement coming from the wife of Rasulullah ﷺ. Secondly, this statement is coming from someone endowed with knowledge, as Rasulullah ﷺ said about Aisha ﷺ, "take *deen* from Aisha." A third, and most important point to highlight is that Syeda Aisha ﷺ did not use the word "like" or "implement" when it came to describe the character of Rasulullah ﷺ in relation to the Quran, but rather she used the word "was"! This shows us that, although we may try hard, we will never reach to the level of Rasulullah ﷺ, as our characters can only attempt to be the Qur'an.

This description of Rasulullah's ﷺ character by Aisha ﷺ helps us to understand what Allah ﷻ said in the Qur'an, when He mentioned in Surah Al-Isra (9): *"Verily, this Quran guides to the straight path and glad tides the Mu'mins who are engaged in virtuous actions of a great reward."* And then relating to Rasulullah ﷺ in Surah Ash-Shura (52): *"Verily, you guide to the straight path."* All of what Allah ﷻ has mentioned here is regarding the greatness of the character of Rasulullah ﷺ in equating it to the Quran.

As such, for all those whom we love, we wish to share three main points from this discussion:

No one can ever reach the level of Rasulullah ﷺ, but we can strive to follow him ﷺ, as that is what Allah ﷻ wants us to do.

Second, the importance of having the best of characters, as Rasulullah ﷺ said in a Hadith, the closest to him are those with the best of characters. Also, in a Hadith narrated by Imam Ahmad ﷫, Rasulullah ﷺ said that the perfect *iman* of a mumin is such that he has a great character, is humble, and he loves people and people love him; and there is no khair in someone who does not love people and people do not love him.

Lastly, to try and learn about Rasulullah ﷺ and his blessed *seerah*, as Allah ﷻ said in Surah Al Ahzab: There is a great example in following Rasulullah ﷺ.

There is a great deal of shame that is shared across the *ummah* for not having a single institution, department or faculty dedicated to the study of the *seerah* of Rasulullah ﷺ. Imam Sakhawi ﷫ mentioned the twenty volumes just listing the names of books about Rasulullah ﷺ, and we do not even speak about *seerah* now!

If we want *khair* we must learn the *seerah*, as Rasulullah ﷺ is the path and the guide!

Allah ﷻ mentioned in Surah Ahle-Imran (30-31): *"Follow me and Allah ﷻ will love you,"* as if Allah ﷻ is saying if you do not follow Rasulullah ﷺ, He will not love you!

As has been mentioned, Rasulullah ﷺ is the path and the guide. If you were to compare this to a room with many doors, the only door that would be open is the door of Rasulullah ﷺ, and the only way to enter the room is following the path of Rasulullah ﷺ to that very door.

In ending, we should remember Imam Ahmad ﷫ and his struggle against Ma'mun with regards to whether the Qur'an was created, as Imam Ahmad ﷫

risked everything, including his life, to uphold that the Qur'an was not created, but rather the word of Allah ﷻ.

May Allah bless you with every *khair* and gather us with Rasulullah ﷺ.

Allahumma salli alaa Syedina Muhammad wa alaa Ahli Syedina Muhammad.

To Know Him ﷺ is to be Shy

3 Rabi ul Thani 1435 - 3 February 2014

We need to understand Allah ﷻ; We need to know Allah ﷻ.

In a Hadith, Rasulullah ﷺ said that Allah ﷻ is the Most Shy, and the Most Covering of the faults of others faults. In another Hadith, Rasulullah ﷺ said that Allah ﷻ is the Most Shy and the Most Generous. He is the Most Shy when His slave raises his hands, as He is shy to return them back empty handed. Normally it is the one who asks that is shy! How wonderful a situation we are in!

Allah ﷻ says in the Qur'an:

Surah Al-Baqarah (185): *"If they ask about me, verily I am very close, and respond to all that ask."*

Surah Al-Ghaffir (60): *"Keep asking me, and I will respond to you."*

Surah Al-Furqan (77): *"Say, Allah ﷻ encourages us to ask from Him."*

All of these *ayahs* should make us realize the Mercy upon us and make us feel shy from Allah ﷻ. We should be shy from Allah ﷻ when thinking about the amount of blessings He has bestowed upon us, reflecting on the sins we have committed, and realizing the extent and level of our *ibadah*.

In this regard, we see the greatness of the Saliheen. Syedina Abu Bakr ؓ said *"Oh Muslims! Be shy from Allah ﷻ."* He was so shy from Allah ﷻ to even raise his head, knowing his natural need to relieve himself.

Fudhail ibn Iyad ؓ said nothing on the day of Arafat out of his shyness; the only thing he did was cry and say that he was ashamed even if he had been forgiven.

Rasulullah ﷺ encouraged us to be shy. Rasulullah ﷺ even mentioned that he was shy from Uthman ؓ, and when asked why, he said *"Should I note be shy from someone that the malaika are shy from?"* ﷺ

May we remember Syedina Zakariyya ؑ, who Allah ﷻ reminds us of in Surah Mariam, when Allah ﷻ mentions His Mercy upon Zakariyya ؑ, and then Zakariyya ؑ asking Allah ﷻ widely. This is to know and understand Allah ﷻ and His Mercy.

May Allah ﷻ open the doors of knowing Him and show us the signs of His Beauty ﷻ.

Allahumma salli alaa Syedina Muhammad wa alaa Ahli Syedina Muhammad.

Jummah Mubarak - *Dua*

6 Jumada 1435 - 7 March 2014

Oh Allah ﷻ, on this blessed day of Jummah, grant us all the *khair*, as Rasulullah ﷺ told us the best day is that of Jummah.

And Ya Allah, as Rasulullah ﷺ told us to make *salawat* during the night and day of Jummah, please allow us to make *salawat* and to receive all the *khair*.

Oh Allah, there are many of Your servants that are going through tribulations, and their hearts and minds remain in unrest. On this day, Ya Rabb, grant them peace in their minds and their hearts.

Oh Allah, there are many of Your servants that are going through various illnesses. On this day, Ya Rabb, they are in need of Your Shifa, so that their hearts, mind and body are cured of all illnesses.

Oh Allah, there are many of Your servants that have knocked on every door and have been rejected and turned away, and the verily the only door that is open is Your door. On this day, Ya Rabb, grant them the opening they have been waiting for. Ya Allah, as You mentioned Your Great Miracle in the Qur'an, that Your Rahma covers everything and all, Ya Rabb, please cover them with Your Rahma.

Ya Rabb, be pleased with us, and gather us with Your Beloved ﷺ. You are the only we ask as You are the only One who can grant our prayers true.

Oh Allah, You said that You and the Malaika send salawat upon Rasulullah ﷺ, and You commanded us to send salawat upon Rasulullah ﷺ, Ya Allah please give us the ability to send our salawat with the best of *adab*. Ya Rabb, as You are the only One who Knows Your Beloved ﷺ, please grant us the ability to send a salawat that is requested through You, raised by You, and thereupon sent to Rasulullah ﷺ.

Allahumma salli alaa Syedina Muhammad wa alaa Ahli Syedina Muhammad, fi kulli lamhatin wa nafasin 'adada maa wa see-a-hu 'il-mullah

Rahma – After Difficulty Comes Ease

8 Jumada 1435 - 9 March 2014

How many instances of *rahma* are hidden from even the smartest of people?

And how much ease comes after a lot of hardship?

Know, this is an opening that comes from a broken heart!

There may be a lot of issues that hurt us in the morning, but by the evening, those same issues are a source of happiness.

The *rahma* of Rasulullah ﷺ is always with us, as long as we are a part of the *"alameen"* (all the worlds).

Allah ﷻ said to Rasulullah ﷺ in Surah *Alamnashra*, *"Did we not open your chest?"* And indeed, the believers are included in this opening!

Allah ﷻ continues by saying *"For indeed, after difficulty comes ease. Indeed, after difficulty comes ease."* Allah ﷻ repeats that for the difficulty there will be two eases.

This is related to when we find it difficult to breathe and our heart may feel constricted because of a sin we have committed, be sure that there is a Nur inside your heart, because if there was not, you would not find it difficult to breathe!

Allahumma salli alaa Syedina Muhammad wa alaa Aali Syedina Muhammad, fi kulli lamhatin wa nafasin 'adada maa wa see-a-hu 'ilmu-LLAH

Shifa

9 Jumada 1435 - 10 March 2014

Bismillah-ir Rahman-ir Raheem.

Allah ﷻ said in Surah Az-Zumar (42): *"Allah takes the ruh of people at the time of their death, and for those who are alive He takes their ruh when they are asleep; and He keeps the ruh of those who have died with Him and gives back the ruh for those that are asleep. In this there is a great sign for those who think and are aware."*

Allah ﷻ is saying sleeping is a minor death, as the *ruh* travels back to Allah ﷻ, and even the *ruh* of a *mu'min* can travel through the *Alam of Malakut*!

Before going to bed, we prepare ourselves, the bed, the room and all this in order to enjoy our sleep is a minor death! In this *ayah*, if the connotation of sleeping is minor death, then we should be wise and prepare for the greater death, the death in which we will lie in our graves.

The way in which we can prepare for our parting is by doing a lot of *ta'a* (worship/obedience) and connecting to the Shifa, Rasulullah ﷺ, in order that we may also enjoy the greater death!

We often wonder that, when we avoid some things or certain foods because it may cause us to become ill, we never think about the *ma'siah* (disobedience) we commit which draws the anger of Allah ﷻ.

We must remember what Allah ﷻ said in Surah Al-Qiyamah (2): *"I swear by the nafs that is blaming;"* blaming the *mu'min* for the *khair* which was missed, the evil that was committed, and not making the most of the time that was allotted.

All the *khair* is from Rasulullah ﷺ. In a Hadith, Hadhrat Omar ؓ recounts that Rasulullah ﷺ said that any Muslim that can bring a witness on the Day of Judgement will enter *Jannah*! The Sahaba ؓ, asked the question (what a mercy their questions are for us!) that what if someone is unable to bring four witnesses, Rasulullah ﷺ replied that they could bring three; the Sahaba ؓ then asked if they were unable to bring three, and Rasulullah ﷺ responded by saying that they could bring two, and the Sahaba ؓ became shy to ask any further [*Sahih Bukhari 1368*].

May Allah ﷻ make us worthy of the Shifa of Rasulullah ﷺ.

Allahumma salli alaa Syedina Muhammad wa alaa Ahli Syedina Muhammad, fi kulli lamhatin wa nafasin 'adada maa wa see-a-hu 'il-muLLAH

In a narration, Al Abbas ﷺ saw Abu Lahab, in hellfire, and he asked him, "What have you encountered?" Abu Lahab said: "I have not found any rest since I left you, except that I have been given water to drink in this (the space between his thumb and other fingers) and that is because of my manumitting of Thuwaiba."

Imam Jamaluddin al Qasimi al Dimashqi ﷺ said:

إذا كان هذا كافر جاء ذمةُ ٭ وتبت يداه في الجحيم مخلدا

Idha kana hatha kafirun ja'aa thamuhu   Wa tabat yadahu fi al jaheemi mukhalada

If this is the state of the disbeliever who has been cursed with "tabbat yada" for eternity in hellfire,

أتى أنه في يوم الاثنين دائماً ٭ يخفف عنه بالسرور بأحمدا

Atah annahu fi yaumi al ithnaaini da'iman   Yu'khafafu annhu bi'sururi bi'Ahmeda

And we are told that his torture is reduced every Monday due to this happiness upon the birth of Ahmad (sallallahu alayhi wasalam),

فما الظن بالعبد الذي كان عمره ٭ بأحمد مسروراً ومات موحدا

fama adha'nu bil'abdi alathee kana umuruhu be'Ahmeda masseruran wa mat muwahida

So what about the one who whose life is happy by Ahmad (sallallahu alayhi wasalam) and who died in iman?

Al Ajwiba al Mardiya (v2, Pg 737) – As Sakahwi
Sahih al Bukhari (v7, Book 62, No. 38)
Explanation of Al Muwahib al Laduniya (v1, Pg 260) – al Zurqani

Run to Him

10 Jumada 1435 - 11 March 2014

In our time, we hear much about having fear of Allah ﷻ, or in other instances having hope. However, what we do not speak about is loving Allah ﷻ! Loving Him, is to, in every situation, to go to Him, run to Him, and to Him and only Him ﷻ!

In Surah Ad-Dhariyat (50) Allah ﷻ says: *"Escape towards Allah."* Flee from everyone other than Allah ﷻ. Run from everything besides Him ﷻ!

What an invitation! An open invitation. When you accept the invitation you enter into *khalwa* (seclusion) without any appointment booking, no allotted time or limit. From the *Rahma* (mercy) of Allah ﷻ, the decision of when to meet is in your hands, despite the fact that we are the ones in need, He ﷻ makes Himself available to us!

If we think about it, when we run towards something, we do not prepare ourselves, or think about what we are going to say or do, we just run! But when we are invited somewhere, we are usually required to formally accept the invitation and to prepare ourselves before going. With Allah ﷻ there is no formality! No thinking! Just running!

No matter the meeting with Him ﷻ, there are no apologies for staying long; He ﷻ loves our *munajaat* (conversation); how Merciful is He ﷻ!

No apologies for what we say, no consequence for constant repetition of the same request, subject or *dua*, rather He ﷻ loves our consistency in asking. How Great is Allah ﷻ!

In Surah Al-Mulk (12), Allah ﷻ says: *"Those who are aware of Allah ﷻ when they are alone, they will be rewarded with forgiveness and an even greater reward!"*

In *khalwa*, we do not to be need smart or clever in what we ask or say, because He knows before we ask. How Great is He ﷻ!

In *khalwa*, there is no need to be embarrassed for becoming teary eyed or your tongue becoming dry; weakness is power and pride in front of Him. How Latif (subtle) You are ﷻ!

In *khalwa*, you can admit your mistakes and faults without any consequences, because He loves you. How Great is He ﷻ!

Lastly, in *khalwa*, you take leave by leaving all issues in His Hands, present and future. You are there to leave everything and all in His Hands ﷻ. How lucky are the people of *khalwa*!

That is why Rasulullah ﷺ used to leave his family and go far into the mountains, to be with Him ﷻ alone in the smallest of spaces!

May Allah ﷻ open the doors of *marifah*.

Allahumma salli alaa Syedina Muhammad wa alaa Ahli Syedina Muhammad, fi kulli lamhatin wa nafasin 'adada maa wa see-a-hu 'il-muLLAH

Illness and its Cure

13 Jumada 1435 - 14 March 2014

I went to the doctor to ask him about my situation, and to ask him if he knows what has happened to me.

He asked me what I am complaining from, and I said do you not see me? Is it not obvious enough? Do you have to see anything more than this?

I am certain you have nothing to help me, as I am not suffering from fever, because the fever is complaining from me!

You asked me to open my mouth to see it, but can you see it? Can you see what I ate is *halal* or *haram*? Can you see my heart? Do you understand my loss of appetite, illness and symptoms I have been collecting? As you move your stethoscope across my chest, did you hear someone reading the Qur'an and sending *Salawat* from their heart, not their tongue?

You say I have no illnesses, but you never answer my questions!

Oh doctor, let me tell you what you cannot see; my illness is from committing a lot of sins, it is not a cold nor cough. What is the cure from sins that tower over me like mountains?

We ask everyone when we become ill, but we never ask about the illnesses that affect our heart.

The Only One Who Knows told us before that we are going to go through this, and He told us the cure. He said: "*Those who have believed and whose hearts are made tranquil by the remembrance of Allah . Unquestionably, by the remembrance of Allah hearts find tranquility.*" (Surah Ar-Ra'ad: 28)

Let us make this Jummah special by sending salawat from the recesses of our heart.

Allah ﷻ commands us to make *salawat* upon the Beloved: "*Verily, Allah and His angels send their blessings upon Rasulullah* ﷺ *, oh you who believe, send your peace and blessings upon him.*" (Surah Al-Ahzab: 56)

Allahumma salli alaa Syedina Muhammad wa alaa Ahli Syedina Muhammad, fi kulli lamhatin wa nafasin 'adada maa wa see-a-hu 'ilmuLLAH

Dua

18 Jumada 1435 - 19 March 2014

Bismillah-ir Rahman-ir Raheem.

Oh Allah ﷻ, You have made us used to Your Generosity, and we have grown up with Your Blessing, and we cannot live without Your Barakat.

Ya Allah ﷻ, You have Taught us what to ask You, and You blessed us with Syedi ﷺ.

Ya Rabbi, You Know that we do not know anything, as You said in the Qur'an in Surah An-Nahl (78): *"Allah ﷻ brought you to life, when you left the womb knowing nothing, and Blessed you with hearing, sight and intellect so that you may be grateful."*

Ya Allah ﷻ, we do not know what is good for us, and we do not know what tomorrow holds. If the most knowledgeable are ignorant, what about us? If the most powerful are weak, then what about us?

Ya Rabbi, Be Pleased with us and Give us what is good for us, as You know what is best so Choose for us, and do not make us choose for ourselves.

You are the Most Generous and the Sustainer. Make our heart constant in Your remembrance and grateful to You.

Ya Rabbi, You taught us in the Qur'an about the very people You Love the most and that You reward them with the best. In Surah Al-Furqan (75): *"Those will be rewarded with the highest maqam in Jannah for their patience and will be greeted with 'Salam.'"*

Ya Allah ﷻ, no one can give us *sabr* but You; Make us from the *sabireen*!

Dear brothers and sisters, let us ask for this *maqam*.

I warn my brothers and sisters not to look down on any *mu'min*, and not to have a bad thought of any *Mu'min*, no matter what their state, as we do not know who is from the *sabireen*. My advice when speaking about a *mu'min* is to speak as if you are speaking about your own self!

And Allah ﷻ Knows best.

May He gather us always with Rasulullah ﷺ.

Allahumma salli alaa Syedina Muhammad wa alaa Ahli Syedina Muhammad, fi kulli lamhatin wa nafasin 'adada maa wa see-a-hu 'il-muLLAH

Heart of Love

12 Jumada al Thani 1435 - 12 April 2014

Bismillah-ir Rahman-ir Raheem.

May Allah ﷻ forgive and cover with His Mercy those who overlook and cover the mistakes and shortcomings of others in order to keep friendships and relationships, and for the continuation of love; And who does not make mistakes?

In Surah Yusuf, Allah ﷻ praised Yusuf ﷺ when his brothers' mistakes came to him and spoke about him negatively and he overlooked his brothers mistakes.

We are in need of true love in this time.

The heart that is able to love and care is that which when others do mistakes it forgives them, looks for excuses for others, cares for others when they are sick, and remembers those that leave leave this *dunya*. May Allah ﷻ be pleased with those who have pure hearts.

Brothers and sisters, *dunya* is nothing. There are some in this *dunya* that live in a small place, have little furniture, little food and perhaps a cup of water, but they have the source of purification; their *dhikr* is their doctor, their pharmacy, their cure.

Those who are obedient to their Lord, they have a richness in their hearts, and are content with what Allah ﷻ has Given them; they are the ones who are lucky and are happy.

If you are one of them, you have everything and you are a master, and thus, you should enjoy this and worship.

If not, know this *dunya* is mischievous, and is not even worth an hour of your time; therefore, make dua and remember the Master ﷺ.

In Surah Al Ahzab, Allah ﷻ mentioned that we need to struggle and follow him ﷺ.

Know that Guidance is in following him,

Jannah is in following him,

Success is in following him,

Love of Allah ﷻ is in following him ﷺ.

May Allah ﷻ make us worthy of following him ﷺ.

Allahumma salli alaa Syedina Muhammad wa alaa Ahli Syedina Muhammad, fi kulli lamhatin wa nafasin 'adada maa wa see-a-hu 'il-muLLAH

Beautiful Hearts

13 Jumada al Thani 1435 - 13 April 2014

Bismillah-ir Rahman-ir Raheem.

Allah ﷻ loves beauty, and the best beauty is the beauty of the heart. Beautiful hearts are those hearts that are able to forgive and love, are always looking for excuses for the faults of others, and they are so beautiful to the extent that they do not know what hate means.

Allah ﷻ teaches us about beautiful hearts from the example of Ibrahim ﷺ, and how he pleaded and argued with Allah ﷻ for the sake of the people of Lut. Ibrahim ﷺ was worried about them. Allah ﷻ sent the angels and glad tided Ibrahim ﷺ about having his own children, but he was still busy finding excuses for the people of Lut. What is this beauty!

Allah ﷻ has praised Ibrahim ﷺ for his wisdom in this regard.

The beautiful heart makes *dua* for others, feels happy in their happiness and feels pain in their pain.

Allah ﷻ mentions these people when He says in Surah Al-Hashr (10): *"And those who came after them, saying, 'Our Lord, forgive us and our brothers who preceded us in faith and put not in our hearts [any] resentment toward those who have believed. Our Lord, indeed You are All Forgiving and Merciful."*

Having a beautiful is one of the greatest gifts, and is also one of the best forms of worship in itself. If only people were to give attention to beautiful hearts.

These hearts are those that when they see a beautiful house, they make *dua* for the dwellers, or when they see any blessing in a person, whether it be work, relationship, or clothing, they make *dua* to put *baraka* in the blessing and to make the person obedient to Allah ﷻ through it. They are those who when they see their brothers and sisters with their spouse, they make *dua* to for the couple to come closer. They are those who, when they see someone committing a sin, they make *dua* to Allah ﷻ to guide them.

The beautiful heart, before going to sleep, forgives everyone, and pleads that no muslim should be punished. These are the beautiful hearts. More than anything what we need are beautiful hearts. Oh Allah ﷻ, bless us with beautiful hearts.

Allahumma salli alaa Syedina Muhammad wa alaa Ahli Syedina Muhammad, fi kulli lamhatin wa nafasin 'adada maa wa see-a-hu 'il-muLLAH

Wisdom

24 Jumada al Thani 1435 - 24 April 2014

Bismillah-ir Rahman-ir Raheem. Allahumma salli alaa Syedina Muhammad wa alaa Ahli Syedina Muhammad.

Allah ﷻ mentioned in the Qur'an the *dua* of Ibrahim ﷺ when he said in Surah Al-Baqarah (129): *"Oh Allah, send them a messenger from among them, who will recite to them Your signs, teach them the Book and Wisdom and purify them."*

Also Allah ﷻ said in Surah Ahle-Imran (164): *"Allah has blessed the believers by sending among them a Messenger from among them, reciting His signs, purifying them and teaching them the Book and Wisdom..."*

In addition He mentioned in Surah Jumaa (2): *"Allah sent among the illiterate a Messenger from them who recites to them His signs, purifies them and teaches them the Book and Wisdom."*

So, we learn wisdom from *Rasulullah* ﷺ, and this is also one of the purposes of sending *Rasulullah* ﷺ.

Wisdom is a great barkaa and a great honor. Ibn Asakir, Aby Shayba and Abu Na'im ﷺ narrate that *Rasulullah* ﷺ said: *"Wisdom is the lost property of the believer, wherever [he or she] finds wisdom they are worthy of benefit from it."* Allah ﷻ said in Surah Al-Baqarah (269): *Allah ﷻ blesses with wisdom whomever He wants,"* and whoever is blessed with wisdom is indeed in *khair*, but no one remembers this except those with great wisdom!

From this *ayah* we learn that teaching and learning wisdom is a great *ni'mah*.

In a Hadith, *Rasulullah* ﷺ also said *"In some poetry there is wisdom,"* encouraging believers to find wisdom wherever it may be.

Saying this, for those whom we love, we will share from the experience of others, from some things that have been collected from our Greatest Teacher. We share this wisdom with those we love for their benefit only, and we ask that this not be forwarded on to anyone.

Our Greatest Teacher mentioned the following wisdoms:

- Son, be careful from making three people cry:

    1) Someone whom you oppressed

    2) An orphan

    3) The elderly

The drops of their tears will not drop on the ground, but rather they will shower you in punishment.

- Do not hurt those that are older than you, and do not cut your relationship with them, because if you are given life, you will eventually be in their position.

- You can hardly notice the difference in color between salt and sugar; you will only know the difference when you taste them.

- And one of the greatest things he mentioned: There will always be hearts that will never hate you no matter how much you ignore them; and there will always be hearts that never love you no matter how much you honor them. Therefore, chose with whom you want to be!

- Friends will never change, it is just that some call people their friends hastily!

- Some people might leave you, but this is not the end of your story, rather, it is the end of their role in your story!

May Allah ﷻ make us from those who learn and benefit from wisdom and may He gather us with Rasulullah ﷺ.

Allahumma salli alaa Syedina Muhammad wa alaa Ahli Syedina Muhammad, fi kulli lamhatin wa nafasin 'adada maa wa see-a-hu 'il-muLLAH

Does Allah ﷻ Love Me?

12 Rajab 1435 - 11 May 2014

Bismillah-ir Rahman-ir Raheem.

This is a question that comes to mind constantly. I thought about it, and it continually stirs me to know if He does.

These very thoughts made me arrive to thinking that there are certain inherent attributes of the slaves that Allah ﷻ loves, and thus began to look in the Qur'an for those very attributes.

In Surah Ahle-Imran (76), Allah ﷻ says He loves the pious ones, *al mutaqeen*. I do not think I am one of them.

In Surah Ahle-Imran (134), Allah ﷻ says He loves the good doers, *al muhsineen*, the people of *Ihsan*; and definitely I am not one of them.

Also in Surah Ahle-Imran (146) Allah ﷻ says He loves those that are patient, *as-sabireen*; and I am so far from being one of them.

In Surah Imran (159), Allah ﷻ says He loves those who rely on Him, *al mutawakaleen*; and Allah ﷻ knows I keep planning – so how can I be one of them?

In Surah Al-Hujarat (9), Allah ﷻ says He loves those who are just, *al muqsiteen*. I oppress myself, so how can I be just with others?

Looking at the ayats above, I know I am not from any one of them, but there is one ayat that gives me hope.

In Surah Imran (31), Allah ﷻ says: "*If you really love Allah ﷻ, than follow Me and Allah ﷻ will love you.*" Wherever I am, no matter what I do, my heart always follows him ﷺ.

And there is one ayat that Allah has left open for everyone, in o Surah Al-Baqarah (222) Allah ﷻ says He loves those who repent, *at-tawwabeen*. Even after disobeying Him, we can have the blessing of His love!

Ask for forgiveness and receive love from Him!

Astagfir-Allah-hil Adheem ala-thee la illaha Ill-lah, huwal Hayyul Qayyum wa tubu Ilay

I seek forgiveness form Allah ﷻ the Greatest, and there is none worthy of worship except Him, the Living, the Eternal, and I repent unto Him.

Allahumma salli alaa Syedina Muhammad wa alaa Ahli Syedina Muhammad, fi kulli lamhatin wa nafasin 'adada maa wa see-a-hu 'il-muLLAH

In the Widsom of Allah ﷻ

24 Rajab 1435 - 23 May 2014

Bismillah-ir Rahman-ir Raheem.

Allah ﷻ said in the Quran, in Surah Al-Isra (11): *"...Allah ﷻ created humans as hasty (beings)."* We as humans want quick results, and this is clearly seen when we make *dua*, we expect that Allah ﷻ will answer us right away!

However, Allah ﷻ has told us that He will respond in the time He deems appropriate.

Thus, Allah ﷻ tells us the stories of the Prophets, such that we might learn from their example.

In one such example, Allah ﷻ tells us the story of Yusuf ﷺ, in which Yusuf ﷺ was put in a cell with two other people. Yusuf ﷺ was clearly the best of the three, as he was a Prophet, the son of Prophet, the grandson of a Prophet, and we know that he was the most beautiful of all human beings (not including Rasulullah ﷺ who contained all of beauty!).

Despite the greatness of Yusuf ﷺ over the other two people in the cell, Allah ﷻ set those two indivi*dua*ls free before Yusuf ﷺ. One of the indivi*dua*ls was freed to become the servant of the king, and the other was killed.

However, Allah ﷻ, in His Wisdom, freed Yusuf ﷺ last, but when he was released, he was released as a master!

Allah ﷻ, from His Mercy, will respond in His Time, which is the best of times, even though we, as humans, keep giving our conditions, requirements and our own timing.

May Allah ﷻ grant us all patience, wisdom and understanding, and may He gather us all with Syedi ﷺ.

Allahumma salli alaa Syedina Muhammad wa alaa Ahli Syedina Muhammad, fi kulli lamhatin wa nafasin 'adada maa wa see-a-hu 'il-muLLAH

Wisdom

27 Rajab 1435 - 26 May 2014

Bismillah-ir Rahman-ir Raheem.

Allah ﷻ said to Rasulullah ﷺ in the Qur'an, speaking about the previous Prophets (Surah Al-An'am, 90): *"Those are the ones whom Allah has guided. So follow their guidance."* This *ayah* is a lesson directed to all of us, not including Rasulullah ﷺ, who does not need to take lesson from their guidance, but rather, it is to His *ummah*.

From this we also understand that we should learn from one another, and that when we learn wisdom, we should share it. Hence, what follows are such wisdoms that we want to share with those whom we love.

Forgiving one another is a blessing. If someone wants to be happy, they should forget about what others say, as people do not realize what they say can be harmful. Also, avoid the people who have hurtful tongues. In a Hadith, Rasulullah ﷺ said the worst of people on the Day of Judgement are those who are avoided out of fear of their tongues.

Another wisdom we learn from is that in a time of sadness, we should strive to be patient; in a time of happiness, we should be grateful; in a time of anger, we should forgive; and when we fail at something, we should stand up, as failing and falling are one in the same.

Everyday is a blessing from Allah ﷻ, and we should not waste this blessing by thinking about tomorrow, the future or by contemplating our past. Allah ﷻ mentions in the Qur'an (Surah Al Hadid, 23): *"...do not regret over what has been missed, and do become overtly excited for that which you have received..."* Just say *tawwakul-alaa-Allah* and move on.

The best of friends, when they see something good in you, they spread that goodness; when they see something bad in you, they hide it; when they see you have something good, they do not become jealous; and when they see you in a difficult moment, they do not leave you alone. The word friend in Arabic is *siddiq*, which comes from the same root as *saddaqa*, which is *sadq*. Hence, friendship is really *sadq* (sincerity truthfulness).

Most people speak about what mood they are in, whether it good or bad. If mood is such an important factor in our lives, then we should not let any of Allah's creation come near it! We should always keep our mood up, and if we do so, we shall always be in *khair*.

Do not regret meeting anyone in your life. If you meet good people, they will make you happy; if you meet bad people, you will get an experience out of it; and if you meet the worst of people, they will teach you a lesson!

If someone overpowers you by being rude and unjust, teach them otherwise with the best of *adab* and wisdom. Every pot smells of what it contains, and everyone spends from what they have; so, teach them how to spend wisely!

You will never see the stars clearly, except when the night is completely dark.

The more you think good of people, the more Allah will make your situation better. The more you wish good for people, the more *khair* you will receive without even knowing which direction it is coming from!

Do not be sad for something you have missed out on, perhaps if you were to have it, it would be the worst thing for you. Trust in Allah, and know that His choice is the best.

Allahumma salli alaa Syedina Muhammad wa alaa Ahli Syedina Muhammad, fi kulli lamhatin wa nafasin 'adada maa wa see-a-hu 'il-muLLAH

Good Thoughts and Reminders

17 Shaban 1435 - 15 June 2014

Bismillah-ir Rahman-ir Raheem.

Allah ﷻ says in the Qur'an, in Surah As-Saffat (87), "*What do you expect of the Lord of the Worlds?*" Abdullah ibn Masud ؓ said about this *ayah*, "*I swear by Allah ﷻ, whatever you think of Allah ﷻ, He will recompense you with.*"

In the most difficult of moments, let us all have a good thought of Allah ﷻ. This not only applies to our thoughts of Allah ﷻ, but related to this, are the thoughts we have regarding all of creation, as all of creation was made by Allah ﷻ.

One of the *saliheen* said to his friends, regarding someone, there is something in my heart that when I interact with him, I am not at peace. His friend agreed. He then said, may be Allah ﷻ has blocked our hearts from the love of the *saliheen*! The *Saliheen* suspect themselves, not anyone else!

My *wasiyah* to those whom I love is to have good thoughts and only beautiful words for all of our relations.

One of our teachers, in fact our Greatest Teacher ﷺ , said if we were to know what people say in our absence, we would not smile. By not knowing, Allah ﷻ has blessed us. Rasulullah ﷺ even used to make dua for protection from knowledge that does not benefit, of which the knowledge of what others say is a part.

Let us be content with what Allah ﷻ has given us. A little water might save a life, and a lot of water might drown someone. When we go thorough moments of *qabd*, or constriction, Allah ﷻ may be asking us for *astaghfar*! We often say we have two lungs, but rather, we forget about the third lung, which tightens, constricts and makes it difficult to breathe. The need of the third lung is not air, but rather the Qur'an is what benefits it, as the Qur'an is what will raise us and intercede for us, and Rasulullah ﷺ warned us not to abandon it.

Do not care what other people say. Worry about what Allah ﷻ thinks of you. If people do not like you, they call you arrogant or say other such things, and when they like you they would say *mashallah* he or she is the best. We must not indulge in the thoughts of others, as we know, they often waver.

When you do a favor upon someone, do not think about the favour you have bestowed, as in reality whatever we do is for Allah ﷻ. Allah ﷻ says in the Qur'an, in Surah Ahle-Imran (195), "*Verily, Allah ﷻ does not waste the deeds of anyone of you, whether male or female.*" Even people forget what we have done for them, but Allah ﷻ never forgets. The example of this is like a lamp; when it is night, we relish in the lamp light, and when daytime comes, we completely forget about it.

Lastly, please remember to send your *salawat* upon Rasulullah ﷺ.

Allahumma salli alaa Syedina Muhammad wa alaa Ahli Syedina Muhammad, fi kulli lamhatin wa nafasin 'adada maa wa see-a-hu 'il-muLLAH

Ramadan Mubarak

30 Shaban 1435 – 28 June 2014

As the first day of Ramadan will be tomorrow, *inshallah*, we wanted to briefly remind ourselves, and those we love, of the blessings and importance of Ramadan.

Out of all the months of the year, the only month that is mentioned by name in Qur'an, is the month of Ramadan.

As we enter this blessed month, we must first start by asking forgiveness from Allah ﷻ, so that we enter the month pure, in order that we may receive blessings from Allah ﷻ, and we must also make our intentions upon entering this month pure.

Ramadan is the month of the Qur'an, the month which contains the night in which Allah ﷻ revealed the Qur'an to Rasulullah ﷺ. As such, we should make this month a month in which we renew and build upon our relationship with the Qur'an.

In Surah Al-Baqarah, Allah ﷻ said He prescribed fasting for us in order that we may achieve *taqwa*. When our stomachs are full, our mind is occupied with other things, making it difficult for us to be occupied only with Allah ﷻ, and therefore, from His Mercy, He prescribed fasting to make it easy for us. May we achieve *taqwa* through our fasting in Ramadan.

Fasting is not only refraining from food and drink, but it is to fast with all of our organs, including our heart, and to not be occupied with anything other than Allah ﷻ!

Ramadan is also the month in which the shayateen are chained, and the doors of *Jannah* are flung open. Allah ﷻ has blessed us with this month as a Month of Mercy, and thus we must strive to make the most of it.

Ramadan is the month in which all of our past *masiyah* are expiated, as Ramadan literally translates to "extreme heat". May this month be a month of cleansing ourselves.

May Allah ﷻ bless your Ramadan with all the *khair*, and may He gather us all with Rasulullah ﷺ.

Ramadan Mubarak

Allahumma salli alaa Syedina Muhammad wa alaa Ahli Syedina Muhammad, fi kulli lamhatin wa nafasin 'adada maa wa see-a-hu 'il-muLLAH

Shukr (Gratefulness) – Part One

8 Ramadan 1435 - 6 July 2014

Bismillah-ir Rahman-ir Raheem.

One of our beloved students asked us about the *maqam* of *shukr*, and its mention in the Qur'an, and about the people of *shukr* and how we can be counted from among them.

To all my beloved brothers and sisters, may Allah ﷻ cover us with His Mercy, we must be aware of the greatness of *shukr*, and its lofty *maqam*, which the Qur'an repeatedly mentions and describes as the highest of *maqams*. We are grateful to Allah ﷻ for His endless blessings and never ending Generosity; a blessing that started before we were aware and a blessing that does not end when we leave this *dunya*!

In the Qur'an, Allah ﷻ commands us to be grateful, and admonishes those who are not. He advises us that His closest slaves are those from the *shakireen*. Not only this, but Allah ﷻ made our purpose of creation *shukr*! *Shukr* carries with it the greatest of rewards, opens the door of more blessing and is what protects and defends the blessings given to us by Allah ﷻ.

Those who benefit from the ayat of Allah ﷻ are the grateful ones!

Allah ﷻ mentions *shukr* many times in the Qur'an, in particular as a command to *shukr*, relating *iman* with *shukr* and with regards to the *maqam* of *shukr*.

Command to shukr

"Then eat of what Allah has provided for you [which is] lawful and good. And be grateful for the favor of Allah, if it is [indeed] Him that you worship." (Surah An-Nahl: 114)

"So remember Me; I will remember you. And be grateful to Me and do not deny Me." (Surah Al-Baqarah: 152)

"You only worship, besides Allah, idols, and you produce a falsehood. Indeed, those you worship besides Allah do not possess for you [the power of] provision. So seek from Allah provision and worship Him and be grateful to Him. To Him you will be returned." (Surah Al-Ankabut: 17)

Shukr and Iman

"What would Allah do with your punishment if you are grateful and believe? And ever is Allah Most Grateful and Knowing." (Surah An-Nisa: 147)

In this *ayat*, Allah ﷻ mentions the *maqam* of *shukr* before *iman*! Allah ﷻ does not punish those who are grateful, but rather, punishment is saved for the ungrateful. At the end of the *ayat*, Allah ﷻ says He is the Most Grateful, which means that He is Grateful for our gratefulness to Him, but does He need our gratefulness? What a Mercy from Allah ﷻ!

The Maqam of Shukr

"And thus We have tried some of them through others that the disbelievers might say, "Is it these whom Allah has favored among us?" Is not Allah most knowing of those who are grateful?" (Surah Al-Anam: 53)

Allah ﷻ has connected increasing in baraka with *shukr*:

"And [remember] when your Lord proclaimed, 'If you are grateful, I will surely increase you [in favor]; but if you deny, indeed, My punishment is severe.'" (Surah Ibrahim: 7)

And any increase from Allah ﷻ has no limit!

Allah has divided man into two groups, grateful and ungrateful. The grateful ones are those whom Allah ﷻ loves, and the ungrateful ones are the ones absent from the love of Allah ﷻ; and Allah ﷻ is in no need of our gratefulness, rather it is for ourselves:

"Indeed, We guided him to the way, be he grateful or be he ungrateful." (Surah Al-Insan: 3)

"If you disbelieve - indeed, Allah is Free from need of you. And He does not approve for His servants disbelief. And if you are grateful, He approves it for you; and no bearer of burdens will bear the burden of another. Then to your Lord is your return, and He will inform you about what you used to do. Indeed, He is Knowing of that within the breasts." (Surah Az-Zumar: 7)

"And We had certainly given Luqman wisdom [and said], "Be grateful to Allah." And whoever is grateful is grateful for [the benefit of] himself. And whoever denies [His favor] - then indeed, Allah is Free of need and Praiseworthy." (Surah Luqman: 12)

"Said one who had knowledge from the Scripture, "I will bring it to you before your glance returns to you." And when [Sulaiman] saw it placed before him, he said, "This is from the favor of my Lord to test me whether I will be grateful or ungrateful. And whoever is grateful - his gratitude is only for [the benefit of] himself. And whoever is ungrateful - then indeed, my Lord is Free of need and Generous." (Surah An-Naml: 40)

The grateful ones to Allah ﷻ are the elite and the chosen ones, and are few in number:

"Then I will come to them from before them and from behind them and on their right and on their left, and You will not find most of them grateful [to You]." (Surah Al-Araf: 17)

"They made for him what he willed of elevated chambers, statues, bowls like reservoirs, and stationary kettles. [We said], "Work, O family of Daud, in gratitude." And few of My servants are grateful." (Surah As-Saba: 13)

"Have you not considered those who left their homes in many thousands, fearing death? Allah said to them, "Die"; then He restored them to life. And Allah is full of bounty to the people, but most of the people do not show gratitude." (Surah Al-Baqarah: 243)

We then must draw our attention to the fact that Allah ﷻ has removed us from the wombs of our mothers and blessed us with senses and intellect, with the only purpose being that we be grateful; in fact, the only purpose of our creation is to be grateful:

"And Allah has extracted you from the wombs of your mothers not knowing a thing, and He made for you hearing and vision and intellect that perhaps you would be grateful." (Surah An-Nahl: 78)

Allah ﷻ even created night and day and gave us sustenance, which are vital for us, so that we may be grateful. If we do not realize that the purpose of our creation is to be grateful, perhaps y looking at what is around us and our sustenance, that will cause us to be grateful:

"And out of His mercy He made for you the night and the day that you may rest therein and [by day] seek from His bounty and [that] perhaps you will be grateful." (Surah Al-Qasas: 73)

"And it is He who subjected the sea for you to eat from it tender meat and to extract from it ornaments which you wear. And you see the ships plowing through it, and [He subjected it] that you may seek of His bounty; and perhaps you will be grateful." (Surah An-Nahl: 14)

Allah ﷻ has also shown us the examples of gratefulness through His Prophets:

"O descendants of those We carried [in the ship] with Nuh. Indeed, he was a grateful servant." (Surah Al-Isra: 3)

"Indeed, Ibrahim was a [comprehensive] leader, devoutly obedient to Allah, inclining toward truth, and he was not of those who associate others with Allah. [He was] grateful for His favors. Allah chose him and guided him to a straight path." (Surah An-Nahl: 120-1)

"[Allah] said, "O Musa, I have chosen you over the people with My messages and My words [to you]. So take what I have given you and be among the grateful." (Surah Al-Araf: 144)

Allah ﷻ blessed us with the best of examples in the Best of Creation ﷺ, which we ought to be grateful for:

In Sahih Bukhari, Rasulullah ﷺ mentioned in a Hadith that he is the most pious and knows Allah ﷻ the most ﷺ!

Saying this, we find in another Hadith narrated by Mughira ibn Shu'ba, that Rasulullah ﷺ used to stand in prayer for such long hours that his feet became swollen. The Sahaba ؓ asked Rasulullah ﷺ why he stood in prayer, since Allah ﷻ has forgiven him for what has past and for what is to come, and Rasulullah ﷺ responded, *"Should I not be a grateful slave of Allah ﷻ?"* Ya Syedi ﷺ Ya Rasulullah ﷺ!

What we have spoken about in this part is the *maqam* of *shukr*, and how Allah ﷻ describes the people of *shukr* in the Qur'an. In the next part, we will discuss what shukr is and how we can be grateful.

May Allah ﷻ make us from among the grateful ones, and may He gather us with Rasulullah ﷺ.

Allahumma salli alaa Syedina Muhammad wa alaa Ahli Syedina Muhammad, fi kulli lamhatin wa nafasin 'adada maa wa see-a-hu 'il-muLLAH

What is *Shukr* (Gratefulness) – Part Two

10 Ramadan 1435 - 8 July 2014

Bismillah-ir Rahman-ir Raheem.

This is the second part of our discussion on *Shukr*. In this part we will describe what *shukr* is and how we can be counted from among the *shakireen*.

What is *Shukr*?

Shukr is to admit to and acknowledge the blessing and the Provider of the blessing with complete humility and love; always knowing that none besides Allah ﷻ can Provide. As such, you must understand the blessing, because if you do not understand the blessing and its importance, you cannot know *shukr*. Also, if you know the blessing but not the Provider, how can you be thankful? If you know both the blessing and the Provider, but do not show humility, love and are not fully pleased with the blessing and the Provider, you will never be grateful.

Thus, we must look at the foundation of *shukr*, namely, five principles:

1) Showing humility to the Provider

2) Love for the Provider and the blessing He has Provided

3) Acknowledgement of the blessing and knowing its importance

4) Praising the Provider by remembering the blessing

5) Not using the blessing given by the Provider for any purpose that He may dislike

These five principles are the foundations of *shukr*; if any one of them is missing, the foundation will be weak.

Shukr is an act of the heart, the tongue and all of our organs:

The act of the heart is the most important, as its role is to show love, humility and *faqr* (complete dependence) towards the Provider.

The tongue's role is to praise the Provider, speak about Him and the blessing He has given you.

The other organs are responsible for being obedient to Allah ﷻ and following Syedi ﷺ, the Master of all of creation.

Imam ibn Abi *Dunya* ؓ wrote a book on *shukr*, in which he mentioned from the *saliheen* a man named Abu Hazim ibn Dinar ؓ. Abu Hazim ؓ said:

To the one who asks how can I do shukr with my eyes, to him say shukr with one's eyes is to spread and speak of the blessings you see and to hide and refrain from that which is not shukr and not from your lot of blessings.

To the one who asks how can I do shukr with my ears, to him say shukr with one's ears is by reporting what one hears that is good and to remove from what you hear that which is not khair.

To the one who asks how can I do shukr with my hands, to him say shukr with one's hands is not to touch or take anything that does not belong to you and to give what is the right of others.

To the one who asks how can I do shukr with my stomach, to him say shukr with one's stomach is such that the bottom of the stomach should be filled with food, while the top be filled with knowledge.

Examples of *shukr* can be seen in the lives of the *saliheen*, which help give us the inspiration and *himma* to strive to achieve this lofty *maqam*:

The Story of Abu Qulaba ﷺ

Ad Dhahabi and Imam Ozai ﷺ narrated that once Muhammad ibn Abdullah ﷺ was going towards the border in the direction of Egypt when he saw a small tent-like structure made out of tree leaves. From within this makeshift tent, he heard a voice. When he went closer, he saw a man that he thought had no blessings; the man had no hands, no legs, was blind and his hearing was very weak. The man was sitting there thanking Allah ﷻ for all of his blessings. He was saying, O Allah, bless me and give me the ability to thank You for all the blessings You have given me." Muhammad ibn Abdullah ﷺ asked him to repeat the *dua* and then asked the man what blessing he was referring to? The man said, "If Allah was to send fire from heaven that can take me, the mountains that can destroy me, the sea that can envelope me or the earth to swallow me, even if He was to do all of that, I would thank Him for the ability to say, 'Alhumdulillah!"

Then the man asked Muhammad ibn Abdullah ﷺ, "Now that you are here, I need your help." He said, "Allah ﷻ has blessed me with a young boy who was serving me and I have not seen him for a few days, can you find him for me?" Muhammad ibn Abdullah ﷺ accepted the request, and set off looking for the boy. He found the young boy, but he had been eaten by animals. Muhammad ibn Abdullah ﷺ was perplexed by what he would tell the man. How could he tell him that his son, the only one who was helping him, died! He forgot about all of the possible explanations and remembered the name of Ayub ﷺ, who Allah ﷻ tested with the death of his children and a disease which turned the people away from him, but yet Ayub ﷺ never stopped thanking Allah ﷻ for all his blessings!

Muhammad ibn Abdullah ﷺ came to the man and told him the story of Ayub ﷺ. The man heard the story and then asked Muhammad ibn Abdullah ﷺ to tell him what he was really trying to say, to which Muhammad ibn Abdullah ﷺ told him that his son had died. The man said,

"Alhumdulillah! What a blessing that none of my children died with sin, as my son has died before the age of maturity!" He then said, "*Ashahadhu an la illaha illlAllah*," and he died. Muhammad ibn Abdullah ﷺ became worried about how he would bury the man alone. It was then that four men came on horses and asked him if he needed anything. When he told them about what had happened, they asked to see the man's face, and upon seeing it, they started kissing him. When they were asked why they were revering the man, they said that this man was the student of Abdullah ibn Abbas ؓ! His name was Abdullah ibn Zaid ؓ and his *kunya* was Abu Qulaba ؓ.

May Allah make us from the *shakireen*, and may He gather us with Rasulullah ﷺ.

Allahumma salli alaa Syedina Muhammad wa alaa Ahli Syedina Muhammad, fi kulli lamhatin wa nafasin 'adada maa wa see-a-hu 'ilmuLLAH

Ramadan Farewell

28 Ramadan 1435 – 26 July 1435

Bismillah-ir Rahman-ir Raheem.

As we are at the end of Ramadan, we say, to those we love, may Allah ﷻ accept our *ibadah*, deal with us with His *Rahma*, and give us what we do not deserve of His blessings.

As we bid farewell to Ramadan, we remember Syedina Imam Hasan al Basri ﷺ who said: *"I know that my rizq is from Allah ﷻ and no one will take it other than me, so I am calm; I know that my actions have been designated for me to perform and no one else, so I busy myself with Him and Him only; I know Allah ﷻ is looking at me, so I am shy to disobey Him; I know death is waiting for me, so I prepare myself and my provisions for that journey."*

As we leave Ramadan, we should be certain that we have a Lord who, if we knock His door when we are in difficulty or in a calamity, His door will always be open! Not only this, but Allah ﷻ encourages us to ask Him.

May Allah ﷻ make us happy always.

What is happiness?

Everyone looks at happiness from their own perspective, but they usually define it as gaining something they may lack.

The patient believes his happiness lies in his cure; the one in financial difficulty thinks their happiness lies in money or removal of their debt; the one without children believes their happiness is in children; and some may believe that freedom from the control of others is where their happiness lies.

However, in reality, happiness is not something you see, or that is necessarily tangible, but rather it is in the heart. If you think something makes you happy, when you get that specific thing, you may encounter another situation that causes you to forget that happiness you received, and instead, it is replaced with concern, stress and anxiety.

Happiness is in the heart, wherever you are.

Happiness is in getting your relationship right with Allah ﷻ. In the Qur'an, with whatever Allah ﷻ mentions, He says to 'tell them' of what He mentioned, but in one *ayah*, Allah ﷻ does not do this. When Allah ﷻ describes how close He is to us, Allah ﷻ does not say 'tell them', it is as if we were not supposed to be, or have the need to be, told this!

Trust in Him, He is the Most Wise!

When I am sick, imagine that my sickness is a source of *rizq* for the doctor, the lab, the X-ray technician, the pharmacy, the taxi driver; by someone's sickness someone gains rizq, and other families benefit. We should look far and wide, and not just at our specific issue or problem, as Allah ﷻ is the Most Wise. We must understand that the solving of our immediate issue may not bring about happiness to us, or to the others that are impacted, positively or negatively, by that immediate issue. Rather, happiness is in knowing Allah ﷻ, and maintaining our relationship with Him, which should be the prevailing constant in our lives.

Understanding this is what we want. Al Hakeem ﷻ, the Most Wise, has tested one person with another. He may have tested me with a wife, daughter, son, parents and neighbors, but he has also tested others with me! Allah ﷻ has created me in their service, and created them in mine.

Allah ﷻ says in Surah Al-Baqarah (251): *"...And if it were not for Allah checking [some] people by means of others, the earth would have been corrupted, but Allah is full of bounty to the worlds."* Thus, order is maintained by this constant test.

We must also realize how Great Allah ﷻ is. All of His attributes were there before we existed. He was Rahim before those who needed it were created, He was Razzaq before *rizq* was created and those who needed it, He was *Karim*, before those who needed His Generosity were created and sought His Generosity!

May Allah ﷻ not deal with us the way we are with others and Him, but rather, may He deal with us in the way He is. May He keep giving us from His blessings, and may we know that this is the reality, the knowledge of which will induce within us everlasting happiness.

May Allah ﷻ make us closer to Him, give us happiness in our hearts and gather us all with Rasulullah ﷺ.

Allahumma salli alaa Syedina Muhammad wa alaa Ahli Syedina Muhammad, fi kulli lamhatin wa nafasin 'adada maa wa see-a-hu 'ilmuLLAH

Your Secret with Him

12 Shawwal 1435 - 8 August 2014

Bismillah-ir Rahman-ir Raheem.

Some people might see you as a pious, good hearted and righteous person, while others may see you as a disobedient, harsh and selfish person; but you know yourself! Do not make a fool out of yourself by thinking of the good things people say about you, and do not feel guilty or bad for what people say about you as well.

The only secret, that no one knows other than you, is your relationship with Allah ﷻ. Do not worry about those who praise you, and do not think about those who think you are evil. None of this will benefit or harm you. Your Lord said in Surah Al-Qiyamah (14), that a person will know him or herself; from the Rahma of Allah ﷻ, He did not put your relationship with Him in public! You might walk into a *masjid* as a *Mu'min*, but what is your *niyah*? You might give *sadaqah*, but what is your *niyah*? People might say a lot of things about you, but no one knows your relationship with Him, He kept this a secret! Love Him, enjoy His company, and increase in your secret with Him ﷻ.

We live between obedience and disobedience, and that is human nature. But this very nature is dangerous, as we do not know whether we will be in a state of obedience or disobedience at the time of our departure from this world. Any form of obedience that Allah ﷻ has chosen you for, appreciate it, respect the moment, and He may allow you to end your existence in this world in obedience. For any form of disobedience, it is not the act of disobedience that should consume us, but rather, knowing that Allah ﷻ has left you to yourself and removed His protection, that is the greatest misfortune!

When we do an act of obedience, do it sincerely out of love, not as a duty. What you give of yourself in love is different than what you do as a duty.

Keep doing the *nafl* (super-obligatory acts) to get closer to Him, and do not do it as a favor to Him! I swear by Allah ﷻ, you need the act of obedience, He does not! Everything you do is for the benefit of yourself.

Do not make your absolute aim the affection of people. Hearts and thoughts change, and love today may be hate tomorrow. The aim should be the love of the Lord of Mankind, because His love means He will never leave you to yourself!

Haram remains *haram*, even if the whole world is doing it. Trust in Allah ﷻ and Rasulullah ﷺ, and remember in Surah Al-Ahzab, Allah ﷻ made Rasulullah ﷺ your example, so follow him and no one else! On *Youm ul Qiyamah*, you will be accounted alone, with no one else, as Allah ﷻ said in Surah Mariam (95): *"And all of them are coming to Him on the Day of Resurrection alone."*

At the end, Allah ﷻ said to Rasulullah ﷺ in Surah Hud (112): *"Be steadfast and follow the straight path as you were Commanded."* Allah ﷻ did not say follow the path as you wish, rather, He said 'Commanded'! Always remember you are a slave. Even when you are following the straight path, know that you were commanded to it. Make a secret between Him and you that no one knows other than Him. As the sin that is committed in secret might destroy you, the obedience done in secret might save you!

May Allah ﷻ allow us to increase in our secret with Him, may He gather us with Rasulullah ﷺ and may He make us worthy of His Shifa.

Allahumma salli alaa Syedina Muhammad wa alaa Ahli Syedina Muhammad, fi kulli lamhatin wa nafasin 'adada maa wa see-a-hu 'il-muLLAH

Husn Dhan

14 Shawwal 1435 – 10 August 2014

Bismillah-ir Rahman-ir Raheem.

Some thoughts we wanted to share with those we love.

Have *husn dhan* (a good thought/impression) and do not follow shaytan by trying to undermine the intention of people, even if the ill intention of someone's actions and words becomes clear to you, still have *husn dhan*. Control your thoughts by making excuses for others. Abdullah ibn Omar ﷺ would make seventy excuses for people, and even after that, if the person's ill intention was still obvious, he would make more excuses for people. This is the school of Rasulullah ﷺ. The *mu'min* tries to find excuses for people, while the *munafiq* always tries to place the blame on people. Having *husn dhan* is something that will be rewarded. Abdullah ibn Omar ﷺ even said that if someone were to use the *deen* or the name of Allah ﷻ to deceive us, even then we would not hold this against them.

When someone knocks on our door or calls us, they want to be in touch with us. When the *adhan* is given, Allah ﷻ wants to be in touch with us!

Syedina Jabir ﷺ said that no one smiled as much as Rasulullah ﷺ. Smiling constantly does not mean that you are always happy with that which is around you, but rather, constant smiling means you are always happy with the Qadr of Allah ﷻ. So keep smiling!

We often face failure in that which we plan, and when this happens, know this is not from us. No one can say that I have everything I want. If you do not have something, know that perhaps Allah ﷻ in His Wisdom is telling you that you are not ready for it, perhaps you are not ready for the responsibility of that thing or that Allah ﷻ has planned something better for you! Be confident in this, and keep smiling!

Rasulullah ﷺ said to the Sahaba in a Hadith narrated in Sahih Muslim: "*Should I not tell you of that which deletes your bad deeds and elevates you in Jannah? To make wudu despite the weather/circumstances, to walk to the masjid, and to wait for the next salah after performing salah.*" If the weather is cold, or the circumstances difficult, there is a way to get closer to Allah ﷻ! To do *wudu* and, as a result, your sleep to go away is better for you than for your *ruh* to go away without praying!

Allah ﷻ loves those who make *istighfar*. Rasulullah ﷺ used to make *istighfar* at least seventy times a day. If our *istighfar* is greater than our complaints, then Allah ﷻ will take away all that causes us complaint!

At the end we say, let us be optimistic. Rasulullah ﷺ told us to be optimistic, and we will get what we want. People often have a pessimistic attitude or approach, but always remember "*La ilaha illallahu wahdahu la shareeka lah, lahul-mulku walahul-hamd, wahuwa AAala kulli shayin qadeer.*" *None is worthy of worship other than Allah* ﷻ, *alone, without any partner, to Him belongs All Sovereignty and Praise and He has power and control over all things.*

Place your trust in Him, and know that He is the source of all *khair*.

May Allah ﷻ gather us all with Syedi ﷺ.

Allahumma salli alaa Syedina Muhammad wa alaa Ahli Syedina Muhammad, fi kulli lamhatin wa nafasin 'adada maa wa see-a-hu 'ilmuLLAH

"...Say 'Allah!' and leave others to their amusement."

21 Dhul Qaidah 1435 - 16 September 2014

"...Say 'Allah!' and leave others to their amusement."

Allah guides to His light whom He wills. (*Surah An-Nur: 35*)

Bismillah-ir Rahman-ir Raheem.

The *Anwar* of the *ayah*: "...Say 'Allah!' and leave others to their amusement." (*Surah Al-Anam: 91*)

Allah is the source of everything.

With Allah we do not regret what we missed yesterday.

With Allah nothing will keep us busy today.

With Allah nothing will worry us tomorrow.

Allah is the Absolutely Sufficient.

With Allah we do not get scared from people.

With Allah we are not afraid of what others are plotting.

With Allah we do not worry about the betrayal of others.

And Allah will Save us.

"...Say 'Allah!' and leave others to their amusement."

With Allah ﷻ no illness can scare us.

With Allah ﷻ old age does not worry us.

With Allah ﷻ even death does not frighten us.

Allah will Protect us.

"...Say 'Allah!' and leave others to their amusement."

With Allah ﷻ poverty does not terrify us,

Nor With Allah ﷻ does humiliation from others.

With Allah ﷻ we are not afraid from harm.

Allah ﷻ is the Absolutely Sufficient.

"...Say 'Allah!' and leave others to their amusement."

With Allah ﷻ there is no anxiety.

With Allah ﷻ there is no sadness or pain.

With Allah ﷻ no one can even dampen a good mood.

Allah ﷻ is our Sponsor and Protector, and He is the One Who gives good company.

"...Say 'Allah!' and leave others to their amusement."

With Allah ﷻ optimism will fill our world.

With Allah ﷻ safety will cover our space.

With Allah ﷻ protection will surround us.

With Allah ﷻ victory will come to us.

And from Allah, Success is our ally, because Allah ﷻ is the Source of Happiness and our Protector.

"...Say 'Allah!' and leave others to their amusement."

Ya Rabbi, oh my Master, oh my Creator, oh my Lord! You said *"I am how My slave thinks of Me, so let My slave think of Me however He wants."* Ya Allah, Your slave does not think of You other than *Khair!* All the *khair* is in Your hands.

Oh Allah, make me and those I love to live in *khair*, to live with *khair*, on the path of *khair*, until we meet You in *khair*!

May Allah bless your day with every *khair*.

Keep sending your *salawat* upon Rasulullah ﷺ, and may He gather us with Syedi ﷺ always.

Allahumma salli alaa Syedina Muhammad wa alaa Ahli Syedina Muhammad, fi kulli lamhatin wa nafasin 'adada maa wa see-a-hu 'il-muLLAH

Once Rasulullah ﷺ was sitting in a room with Aisha ﷺ and fixing his shoes. It was very warm, and Aisha ﷺ looked to his blessed forehead and noticed that there were beads of sweat on it. She became overwhelmed by the majesty of that sight, staring at him long enough for him to notice. He ﷺ said, *"What is the matter?"* She replied, *"If Abu Kabir Al-Huthali, the poet, saw you, he would know that his poem was written for you."* Rasulullah ﷺ asked, *"What did he say?"* She replied, "Abu Kabir said:

وَمُبَرَّإٍ مِنْ كُلِّ غُبَّرِ حَيْضَةٍ * وَفَسَادِ مُرْضِعَةٍ وَدَاءٍ مُغِيلٍ

Wa Mubara'aun min kulli ghabrati haidhaten * Wa fasadi mur'diaten wa da'ee mugheli

فَإِذَا نَظَرْتَ إِلَىٰ أَسِرَّةِ وَجْهِهِ * بَرَقَتْ كَبَرْقِ الْعَارِضِ الْمُتَهَلِّلِ

Fa itha nadhartah illa asserati wajhi'he baraqat ka'barqi al aridhi al mutahalili

'that if you looked to the majesty of the moon, it twinkles and lights up the world for everybody to see."

So the Rasulullah ﷺ got up, walked to Aisha ﷺ, kissed her between the eyes, and said, "Wallahi ya Aisha, you are like that to me and more."

The Source of Happiness

26 Dhul Qaidah 1435 - 21 September 2014

"Allah guides to His Light whom He wills." (Surah An-Nur)

Bismiallah-ir Rahman-ir Raheem.

Allah ﷻ said, speaking to Rasulullah ﷺ, in the beginning of Surah TaHa: *"We did not send the Qur'an down to you so that you may be distressed."*

In understanding this *ayah*, we use a ruling from a field of knowledge called *usul ul fiqh*, namely *mahfum al mukhalafah*: that which is *haram* the opposite of it is *halal*, and that which is not recommended, the opposite of it is recommended.

Thus, in the *ayah*: *"We did not send the Qur'an down to you that you may be distressed,"* the opposite of this would be: verily, We sent the Qur'an to make you happy!

The purpose of the *deen* is to be happy in *dunya* and in *al akhira*.

In a Hadith narrated in ibn Majah and by Imam Ahmad ﷺ, Abu Hurrairah ﷺ narrates that Rasulullah ﷺ used to love optimism. Hence, we must be content and happy.

The two things that hurt people and cause them pain are: the pain of what has occurred in the past; and concern for what others say or think.

Allah ﷻ speaks about the past, and the fact that this is something we cannot change, as it was written before we existed. In Surah Al-Hadid (22-23): *"No calamity strikes upon the earth or among yourselves except that it is written before We bring it into being – indeed that, for Allah, is easy; in order that you do not despair over what has been missed and you do not get excited over what He has given you. And Allah does not like those who are self-deluded and boastful."*

In a Hadith narrated in Abu Dawud and by Imam Ahmad ﷺ, ibn Dalaimi ﷺ mentions that he had some issues in his heart regarding the acceptance of the *qadr* of Allah ﷻ, and as he was finding it hard to accept, he went to ask Ubay in Kab ﷺ. In answering the concerns of ibn Dalaimi ﷺ, Ubay ibn Kaab ﷺ said:

"If Allah ﷻ were to punish the people of the heavens (meaning the angels) and earth, this would be more than they deserve, and if He were to be Kind and Merciful, that which He is, that is more than they deserve. If a mountain of gold the size of Uhud were spent for the sake of Allah ﷻ, it would not be accepted unless one believes in the qadr of Allah ﷻ. What is meant for you will never be missed, and what has been missed was never meant for you."

Ibn Dalaimi ﷺ then went to Abdullah ibn Masud ﷺ and asked about qadr, and he mentioned what Ubay ibn Kaab ﷺ mentioned. Ibn Dalaimi ﷺ then went to Hudaifah ibn al Yaman ﷺ, and he mentioned what Abdullah ibn Masud ﷺ had mentioned about qadr. Ibn Dulaimi ﷺ then went to Zayd ibn Thabit ﷺ, and he mentioned what Hudaifah ibn al Yaman ﷺ had mentioned regarding qadr.

Look at the sahaba and how all four had answered the same; this is the school of Syedi ﷺ! No matter what you may have thought or done, nothing would or will be different from the qadr of Allah ﷻ. This for us is a source of calm and contentment; to be pleased with Allah ﷻ and content.

Allah ﷻ has mentioned in four *ayahs* of the Qur'an "Allah was pleased with them and they were pleased with Allah." Allah ﷻ mentioned this group of people in Surah Al-Mujadala (22), when He called them the Party of Allah ﷻ. He also named this group the People of *Jannah* in Surah Al-Maidah (119), Surah Al-Bayyinah (8) and Surah At-Tawbah (100).

This means we should be pleased with Allah ﷻ and content, as that is the way to His nearness. We cannot change the past; we must accept the past as the clock can never be turned back. Thinking about the past causes anger and bad judgment. Even when the thoughts of the past come up, we must run to Allah ﷻ, as we know, that it is mentioned in the Qur'an, that peace and tranquility only comes from Allah ﷻ and His remembrance.

Regarding the second point, the concern for others and what they say or think; concerning yourself with others only happens to those who are busy with everyone but Allah ﷻ. Because about Himself He said in Surah Az-Zumar (53): *"O My slaves who have transgressed against themselves, do not despair of the Mercy of Allah. Indeed, Allah forgives all sins. Indeed, it is He who is the Forgiving, the Merciful."*

When we think about Him, there is only peace. When we think about other than Him, it only brings sadness. When we try to please others, we only encounter sorrow.

Shaykh Abdul Qadir Jilani ﷺ said in his book, Fath ul Rabbani: *"The more we think about others, the further we go away from Allah ﷻ, and these thoughts are the source of stress."*

My advice for everyone is that the only cure and way out from all the stress is to think about Him, to be pleased with Him, and to be content with Him ﷻ. The result of this is the closeness, pleasure and contentment of Allah ﷻ.

May Allah ﷻ bless you and keep us all in the company of Allah ﷻ and Syedi ﷺ.

Allahumma salli alaa Syedina Muhammad wa alaa Ahli Syedina Muhammad, fi kulli lamhatin wa nafasin 'adada maa wa see-a-hu 'il-muLLAH

The Blessing of the Ten Days of Dhul Hijjah

5 Dhul Hijjah 1435 - 29 September 2014

Allah ﷻ guides to His Light whom He wills."
(Surah An-Nur)

Bismillah-ir Rahman-ir Raheem.

The Blessing of the Ten Days of Dhul Hijjah

The life of a Muslim is very special as it is full of opportunities to get closer to Allah ﷻ by doing the various forms of *ibadah* that Allah ﷻ loves. These forms of *ibadah* turn the life of a Muslim into a life of righteous action, speech and continuous activity for the benefit and goodness of everyone. This means that the life of Mu'mins should be devoted to *ibadah*, obedience, righteous deeds and absolute connection with Allah ﷻ in every part of their life, and in all their affairs. They do not need to go to the *masjid*, in particular, to approach Allah ﷻ, as He is with them all the time, as He said in the Qur'an (Surah Qaf: 16): "...and We are closer to him than [his] jugular vein." From this we know that our life cannot be cut off from the Rahma of Allah ﷻ. So, from having this connection, during the five prayers that are spread over twenty-four hours, the special day of jummah once a week, fasting every year during the month of Ramadan, fasting the six days of Shawwal, fasting on Monday and Thursday every week, fasting the three bright days every month, and then, add to this, the ten days of Dhul Hijjah; those days in which every good deed we do, not only are we rewarded for them, but Allah ﷻ loves good deeds in these days more than any other time of the year.

What is special about the Ten Days of Dhul Hijjah?

The special *ibadah*, *Hajj* is particular to these ten days, and Rasulullah ﷺ said if Allah ﷻ accepted the *Hajj* of someone, they go back from their *Hajj* as a new born baby. Umrah is also performed in these days. For those who do not go for *Hajj*, they can fast for the first nine days, give *sadaqah*, and they can do much from the various types of ibadah. Ibn Hajr ﷺ said that "during these ten days you can do all the major forms of *ibadah*, but this is not possible to gather in any other set of days."

So our life and our striving does not stop anywhere, and no limit for closeness to Allah ﷻ. There is no limit to *qurb*!

Speaking of having no limit to closeness with Allah ﷻ, Surah Alam Nashrah alludes to the maqam of Rasulullah ﷺ :

- *Did We not expand your breast?* – Rasulullah ﷺ is absolutely Rahma!

- *And raised high for you your repute.* - Whenever Allah ﷻ is mentioned the name of Rasulullah ﷺ is mentioned!

- *And to your Lord direct [your] longing!* Keep striving in your connection with Allah ﷻ as there is no limit to closeness!

The Virtues of the Ten Days of Dhul Hijjah in the Qur'an and Sunnah

Qur'an

In Surah Al-Fajr (1-2), Allah ﷻ swears by the time of Fajr and by the ten days, and for Allah ﷻ to swear by something is to elevate its stature to greatness. Ibn Abbas, ibn Zubayr, Mujahid and others ﷺ all agree that the mention of the ten days is those first ten days of Dhul Hijjah.

In Surah *Al-Hajj* (28), Allah ﷻ says: "*...remember the name of Allah* ﷻ *in the known days...*" ibn Abbas ؓ mentions that the days referred to in this *ayah* are the ten days of Dhul Hijjah.

Sunnah

In a Hadith narrated by ibn Abbas ؓ, Rasulullah ﷺ said that *"The best days that Allah* ﷻ *loves good deeds the most in are these days, meaning the ten days of Dhul Hijjah."* (Abu Dawud 2438)

Also in a Hadith narrated by Syedina Jabir ؓ, Rasulullah ﷺ said: *"[of] the ten best days, the tenth is the day of sacrifice (Adha), and the uneven numbered day is the day of Arafah, and these are the ten days of Dhul Hijjah."* (Imam Ahmad)

Also in another Hadith, Syedina Jabir ؓ narrates that Rasulullah ﷺ said that there are *"no days better than the ten days of Dhul Hijjah."* (Ibn Hibban 3853)

Ibn Abbas ؓ narrates that Rasulullah ﷺ said: *"the best of deeds to Allah* ﷻ*, that which He loves and rewards greatly and generously, are those actions performed in the ten days of Dhul Hijjah."* (Sunan al Darimi 1774)

In a Hadith, the Sahaba ؓ asked Rasulullah ﷺ if the *mujahid* could compare to the one who worships in these ten days, to which Rasulullah ﷺ responded that no one can compare to the person who worships in these ten days except for the mujahid who gives away everything he owns and takes what remains with him and leaves it all on the battlefield, including his life. Only this person can compare to the one who worships in these ten days!

The Uniqueness of the Ten days of Dhul HIjjah

The below are some of the unique attributes of the first ten days of Dhul Hijjah:

- Allah ﷻ in Surah Al-Fajr (1-2) swears by the ten days of Dhul Hijjah

- Allah ﷻ mentions in Surah Al-Hajj (28) that these are the most well known days by all, and that we should remember His Name during these ten days

- In a Hadith narrated by Abdullah ibn Omar ﷺ, Rasulullah ﷺ said that there are no days in the year that are greater, and Allah ﷻ loves good deeds in these days (Imam Ahmad)

- Yaum ul Tarwiyyah: This is the eight day of Dhul Hijjah. This is the day that rest was taken by Rasulullah ﷺ in Mina, and where the Hujjaj drank water. Although this is adjacent to Arafat, we follow the *Hajj* of Rasulullah ﷺ, who stopped here for rest with His Companions, who at that time, did not enjoy the facilities we enjoy today

- The Day of Arafah. This is a day to be proud of as Muslims, as this is the day Muslims all gather at the same place. In a Hadith, Aisha ﷺ narrates that Rasulullah ﷺ said: "*There is no other day that Allah ﷻ frees more slaves from jahannaum than the day of Arafah! Allah ﷻ says to His angels on that day, 'Look at My slaves!*'" (Muslim 3288)

- Laylatul Jamiah: After the day of Arafah, the Hujjaj are commanded to go to the "sacred place", which is Muzdaliffah. Here, the *salah* of Maghirib and Isha are combined, and the night before Eid ul Adha is spent here

- *Hajj*: The major *ibadah* that can only be performed in these ten days

- Yaum un-Nahr: The day of Eid ul Adha, in a Hadith it is mentioned as the best day of the year

- Yaum al-Qarr: Day after Eid, which is spent in Mina, and literally means the day of stability

Advice for the Ten Days of Dhul Hijjah

It is not too late to avail the *khair* of the ten days of Dhul Hijjah!

You can start by making constant *tawbah*. Practically, *tawbah* is made of three parts:

1) To depart from that which you were doing or committing

2) Determination: to have the resolve to strive towards Allah ﷻ and to leave what you have left behind

3) To return the rights to people: in case you have wronged anyone, to attempt to do right by those you have wronged

The second action we can do to attract *khair* in the ten days of Dhul Hijjah is to make a righteous intention. We can always make a righteous intention, and our intention should be that we do not want to waste any time in these ten days. We should aim high with our intentions, as the actions themselves are under the control of Allah ﷻ. Many people have surpassed those who do much *ibadah* just with their intention!

In a Hadith, Rasulullah ﷺ said there are four types of people:

1) Those with a good intention who do not complete the action they intended; they will be rewarded for their good intention

2) Those with a good intention who complete the action they intended; they will be rewarded for their intention and the action

3) Those with a bad intention but who do not commit the action they intended; they will be rewarded for their inaction

4) Those with a bad intention who do commit the action they intended; they will be accounted for their action

Based on this, at the minimum, three-fourths of our time is in *khair*! We are not even accounted for our ill intention if we do not act. This is the Mercy of Allah ﷻ!

Best Actions for the Ten Days of Dhul Hijjah

1) *Nawafil*: try to do as many *nawafil salah* as you can, as it is a mentioned in a Hadith that a person's maqam is raised and that bad deeds are erased with each *sujood*.

2) Fast as much as you can. It is mentioned in a Hadith, when a companion asked what the best of deeds was, Rasulullah ﷺ said it is to fast.

3) *Qiaym ul Layl*. Night prayers should be encouraged in these ten days. Abdullah ibn Salam ﷺ mentioned that when Rasulullah ﷺ came to Madinah with all his radiance he mentioned three things to the community: spread *salam*, feed people, and pray while others are asleep. Normally, after such a migration, people would be sceptical and cautions of others, but instead Rasulullah ﷺ summarized the *deen* upon his arrival in Madinah al Munawarrah. The great tab'ee Said ibn Jubayr ﷺ said in the first ten nights of Dhul Hijjah, do not turn off your lights!

4) *Tahlil, Tahmeed, Takbeer*: To repeat *La ilaha illallah, Alhamdulillah and Allahu Akbar – La ilaha illallah – wAllahu Akbar wa Lillaahi'l-hamd*. Abdullah ibn Omar and Abu Hurrairah ﷺ were known for reciting *takbeer* in the market place. Abdullah ibn Omar ﷺ would keep reciting his *dhikr*, and would only return *salam* in these ten days.

5) Day of Arafah: The day of Arafah should be occupied with *dua* and *tawbah*. The life of Rasulullah ﷺ was *dua*, to remember Allah ﷻ with every action in every moment.

The *Dua* on the Day **of Arafah of Syedina Ali** ؓ *karamallah wajhah.*

In making *dua* on the day of Arafah, Syedina Ali ؓ used to repeat the following *dua*:

Oh Allah! Free me from the hellfire.

Ya Allah! Grant me abundant halal rizq.

Ya Allah! Keep away from me the disobedient ones, whether they be jinn or human.

Practically, on the day of Arafah, you should try to take off from work if possible, that way you can spend your day in *dua*. In addition, sleep directly after Isha the night before, and wake up an hour before Fajr in order to be present at the time Allah ﷻ loves to accept *dua*. Make the intention to make this a different day of Arafah; make it a day that is different from all the rest.

In closing, it is important to remind ourselves of the purpose of our *deen*, as is stated in Surah Al-Anbiya: "*We did not send you other than to be a Mercy to all the Worlds,*" speaking about Rasulullah ﷺ. So we can never stop striving, we must be that mercy.

May Allah ﷻ grant us His Mercy and the company of His Mercy ﷺ, and may He make these ten days those of forgiveness and acceptance of our *duas*.

Munajaat

13 Dhul Hijjah 1435 – 7 October 2014

"Allah guides to His Light whom He wills." (Surah An-Nur)

Bismillah-ir Rahman-ir Raheem.

Ya Allah! I am very weak, and no one other than You can provide me strength.

Ya Allah! I gave up trust in myself, but not in the Certainty in You.

Ya Allah! No one other than You can Guide me.

Ya Allah! I am drowning, and no one other than You can save me.

Ya Rabbi! In my moment of weakness, as there are many, I need Your Mercy.

Keep shaytan and my *nafs* away from me, and Guide my heart and mind for me.

Ya Allah! Forgive my sins, mistakes and faults.

Ya Rabbi! Who else am I going to complain to, while You are there. Who else am I going to cry to, while Your door has never closed. Who else am I going to ask, worship and beg, when You alone are worshipped. Who else am I going to place hope in, while my hope in You knows no limit!

Ya Rabbi, Ya Rabbi, Ya Rabbi!

Keep us in Your Forgiveness always, and be Pleased with me in every moment. Make me full of regrets for all my sins, and make me stand at the Door of *Tawbah*.

Ya Allah!

Do not make anything difficult, as there is no difficulty that You cannot make easy.

Do not make anything seem great to me, as there is nothing Great but You.

Ya Rabbi, Ya Rabbi, Ya Rabbi!

Do not make me look down or be shy from anyone other than You.

Ya Allah! Do not reveal my secrets to anyone.

Oh Allah, if I commit a sin openly, forgive me

Oh Allah, if I commit a sin in secret, cover me.

Ya Allah! Do not make my test in my *deen*, and do not allow the *dunya* to be the dominating component of my life.

Ya Allah! Do not test me in my body, sustenance, family or loved ones. You know my weakness, and You are the Most Powerful.

Ya Allah! Do not put those who are jealous of me in charge of my affair, and do not make my enemies elated by any element of my failure.

Ya Allah, Ya Allah, Ya Allah!

The earth has become narrow, even though it is a wide expanse; open it with your *Rahma* like you opened for Yunus ﷺ inside the fish.

Oh Allah, bless us and sustain us and provide for us the happiness of Yaqub ﷺ, the courage of Yunus ﷺ, the *taqwa* of Yusuf ﷺ the sabr of Ayub ﷺ, the *iman* of Musa ﷺ, the tolerance of Nuh ﷺ, the purity of Isa ﷺ and the *Anwar* and *Baraka* of Syedi Rasulullah ﷺ, the Master of all of Creation.

Moments of Happiness: A Gift from Allah ﷻ

22 Dhul Hijjah 1435 – 16 October 2014

"Allah ﷻ guides to His Light whom He wills." (Surah An-Nur)

Bismillah-ir Rahman-ir Raheem.

Rasulullah ﷺ said in a Hadith that there are moments of inspiration and baraka, so make the most of them! *(narrated by Syed Muhammad ibn Maslamah, At-Tabarani: 2398).*

Allah ﷻ said, in Surah Al-Balad (4): *"We created mankind in difficulty."* Our beginning starts with the difficult time of birth, which is difficult for mother and child, we face difficulty when we learn to walk, difficulty at the persistence of our first tooth, difficulty in breast feeding, difficulty in relationships, and this difficulty continues until we leave this *dunya*.

So when we encounter these moments of inspiration, baraka, joy and happiness, we should make the most of them by being grateful to Allah ﷻ, as He said in Surah Ibrahim (7): *"If you are grateful, I will surely increase you..."*

May Allah ﷻ be pleased with our Greatest Teacher ﷺ, who said:

"Do not squander moments of happiness by worrying how long they will last or by remembering the past."

When Allah ﷻ blesses you with that moment of happiness, He wanted you to be happy!

"Do not waste the present by being pessimistic."

Allah ﷻ is the One who knows the *khair*, and that which *khair* for us.

As Allah ﷻ said in a Hadith Qudsi: *"I am as my slave thinks of Me, so let my slave think of Me as they want."*

In fact in another Hadith, narrated in Muslim: *"No one should die except with having a good thought of Allah ﷻ."*

Also in Surah Al Fath, Allah ﷻ blamed those who have a negative outlook on the future, such negative thoughts imply that they have a bad thought of Allah ﷻ.

"Do not waste moments of success by arrogance."

As you did not achieve the success by yourself; Allah ﷻ is the One who granted you the success!

In a Hadith, narrated by Abdullah ibn Masud ﷺ, Rasulullah ﷺ said anyone who has even half of an atom of arrogance in their heart will not enter *jannah*.

"Do not waste the happiness of others by disparaging their moment of happiness."

"Do not waste your day by thinking of yesterday."

Rasulullah ﷺ said that bringing happiness to the heart of someone is *sadaqah*!

Allah ﷻ has given us that which we have never thought of, therefore we must trust Him!

He ﷻ will not stop giving that which we want, except that it is *khair*, and *khair* for us is not getting what He did not give!

May Allah ﷻ gather us with Rasulullah ﷺ with the Baraka of the Saliheen.

Allahumma salli alaa Syedina Muhammad wa alaa Ahli Syedina Muhammad, fi kulli lamhatin wa nafasin 'adada maa wa see-a-hu 'il-muLLAH

Humility

23 Dhul Hijjah 1435 – 17 October 2014

"Allah guides to His Light whom He wills." (Surah An-Nur)

Bismillah-ir Rahman-ir Raheem.

Allah ﷻ when He speaks about Rasulullah ﷺ He speaks about his character and how Great it is.

Think about Allah ﷻ when HE says it is great!

He knows that whatever we do we cannot get to that level, but Allah ﷻ said He made Rasulullah ﷺ the greatest example. (Surah Al-Ahzab)

From the character of Rasulullah ﷺ, we see his humility, tawaba, which literally means something very high that needs strength to come down, as if a tall person is trying to fit through a small door.

In a Hadith, narrated by Abbas ibn Rabiah ؓ, Rasulullah ﷺ said whoever is humble towards Allah ﷻ, Allah ﷻ will raise; the the humble one is the one who believes that he is the lowest, and in the eyes of others he is actually the greatest. If a person is arrogant, Allah ﷻ will lower him no matter where he is, and people will see him lowly as well. (Musnad Shihab)

Rasulullah ﷺ was given the choice of either being a King and a Prophet or a Slave and a Prophet and Prophet, and Syedi ﷺ chose the later. Despite having the choice, Rasulullah ﷺ did not take it!

It was Rasulullah's ﷺ honor to be the slave of Allah ﷻ! In his *dua*, Syedi ﷺ used to say: *"I am your slave, son of your slave and Your Qada and Hukm will happen to me without my choice!"* Just compare this to our lives; as many of us strive for status and fame,

Rasulullah ﷺ, when given the choice, chose slavehood. His humility is beyond our imagination!

In a Hadith narrated by Abu Hurrairah ؓ, Rasulullah ﷺ wanted to buy trousers, but the owner of the shop wanted to kiss the blessed hands of Rasulullah ﷺ, but Rasulullah ﷺ said this is for kings! Abu Hurrairah ؓ then wanted to carry the goods of Rasulullah ﷺ, but Rasulullah ﷺ said people should carry their own things.

In the house of Rasulullah ﷺ, he used to repair his own shoes, clothes and used to help others with their chores.

In a journey with the Sahaba, they had a sheep which they intended to cut, clean and cook, and Rasulullah ﷺ said he would gather the wood, the hardest job of all! The Sahaba said to Rasulullah ﷺ that they would collect the wood, but Rasulullah ﷺ wanted to show that he is similar to them, as a human, even though he is very different!

Brothers and sisters, if you cannot be like the Saliheen, at least try to look like them, as even in their emulation there is success.

Our Our Greatest Teacher ﷺ said:

"**If you want to emulate something, be like the stars, even though they remain high, they can even be seen in the water. Do not be like the smoke, it rises, but it is empty nothingness.**"

This is from the openings of the Saliheen!

May Allah ﷻ Guide us and Keep us in the Nur and Hidayah of Rasulullah ﷺ.

The real struggle is to know you are nothing: at the start you are nothing but fluid, and at the end a rotten body in the ground. No matter how big you become, you will never conquer the size of a mountain; no matter how strong you are, you can never outstand the ground.

Allah ﷻ said he created humans in absolute weakness. A single virus can change the entire life of someone!

Hence, humility is not trying to be something, but rather it is understanding yourself!

May Allah ﷻ Guide us by the Nur, through the Nur and to the Nur.

The Reality of Life

26 Dhul Hijjah 1435 – 20 October 2014

"Allah guides to His Light whom He wills." (Surah An-Nur)

Bismillah-ir Rahman-ir Raheem.

Allah ﷻ said in Surah Al-Hadid (20), speaking about the reality of the *dunya*:

Know that the life of this world is but amusement and diversion and adornment and boasting to one another and competition in increase of wealth and children - like the example of a rain whose [resulting] plant growth pleases the tillers; then it dries and you see it turned yellow; then it becomes [scattered] debris. And in the Hereafter is severe punishment and forgiveness from Allah and approval. And what is the worldly life except the enjoyment of delusion.

This is the reality of *dunya*!

No one can see this reality, even those who expound on its reality, in actuality, work hard for this *dunya*. Even those who urge not to chase *dunya*, they will, on certain occasions based on circumstance, find exception.

When speaking to Sidi Shaykh Hamid ﷺ, I once asked him that we always mention *dunya* and its temporal and abased nature, and Allah ﷻ describes this for us in the Qur'an, but is there anything that can make this clear? Syedina Shaykh Hamid ﷺ said: "You can see the true reality of this *dunya* only after you leave it! However, if you want to see the reality of this *dunya* while you are alive, look at people you know who died; look at those who loved them and see how they leave them when they are buried. You see people walk away from those they loved and forget about them. Remember the same *dunya* that Hamid and Faid talk about will not leave them to themselves. The reality will become clearer if you orient your entire life to Allah ﷻ. He is the only One who does not forget you! He is the One we rely on, and He is the All Powerful and the Ever-Lasting!"

To those whom I love, may we:

Breathe by LA ILAHA ILLALLAH!

In times of pain, say ALHAMDULILAH!

Wonder by SUBHANALLAH!

Admonish ourselves by ASTAGHFIRULLAH!

Begin by BISMILLAH!

Be happy by sending SALAWAT UPON SYEDI ﷺ!

And end by ALHAMDULILAH!

May Allah ﷻ be pleased by you and I, and may He gather us always with Rasulullah ﷺ.

Allahumma salli alaa Syedina Muhammad wa alaa Aali Syedina Muhammad, fi kulli lamhatin wa nafasin 'adada maa wa see-a-hu 'ilmu-LLAH

Quran References:

Surah Ad-Dhariyat: 50	Surah Al-Fajr: 20	Surah An-Nisa: 113
Surah Ad-Dhariyat: 55	Surah Al-Fatih: 28	Surah An-Nisa: 147
Surah Ahle-Imran: 134	Surah Al-Furqan: 75	Surah An-Nur: 15
Surah Ahle-Imran: 146	Surah Al-Furqan: 77	Surah An-Nur: 35
Surah Ahle-Imran: 159	Surah Al-Ghaffir: 60	Surah An-Nur: 62-64
Surah Ahle-Imran: 164	Surah Al-Ghashiyah: 21-22	Surah Ar-Ra'd: 20
Surah Ahle-Imran: 173	Surah Al-Hadid: 20	Surah Ar-Ra'd: 28
Surah Ahle-Imran: 191	Surah Al-Hadid: 22	Surah Ash-Shura: 219
Surah Ahle-Imran: 195	Surah Al-Hadid: 23	Surah Ash-Shura: 40
Surah Ahle-Imran: 30-31	Surah Al-Hajj: 28	Surah Ash-Shura: 52
Surah Ahle-Imran: 76	Surah Al-Hashr: 10	Surah As-Saba: 13
Surah Ahle-Imran: 81	Surah Al-Hashr: 9	Surah As-Saffat: 75
Surah Al-Adiyat: 8	Surah Al-Hujarat: 9	Surah As-Saffat: 87
Surah Al-Ahzab: 56	Surah Al-Insan: 3	Surah At-Tawbah: 100
Surah Al-An'am: 90	Surah Al-Isra: 11	Surah At-Tawbah: 119
Surah Al-Anam: 53	Surah Al-Isra: 3	Surah At-Tawbah: 124
Surah Al-Anam: 91	Surah Al-Isra: 86	Surah At-Tawbah: 36
Surah Al-Anfal: 2	Surah Al-Isra: 9	Surah Az-Zumar: 42
Surah Al-Ankabut: 17	Surah Al-Jumaa: 2	Surah Az-Zumar: 53
Surah Al-Araf: 144	Surah Al-Layl: (4-7)	Surah Az-Zumar: 7
Surah Al-Araf: 17	Surah Al-Luqman: 12	Surah Hud: 112
Surah Al-Araf: 204	Surah Al-Maidah: 119	Surah Ibrahim: 7
Surah Al-Balad: 4	Surah Al-Maidah: 15	Surah Mariam: 23
Surah Al-Baqarah: 129	Surah Al-Mujadala: 22	Surah Mariam: 95
Surah Al-Baqarah: 152	Surah Al-Mulk: 12	Surah Muddathir: 6
Surah Al-Baqarah: 158	Surah Al-Qalam: 4	Surah Muhammad: 17
Surah Al-Baqarah: 177	Surah Al-Qasas: 73	Surah Qaf: 16
Surah Al-Baqarah: 185	Surah Al-Qiyamah: 14	Surah Sad: 30
Surah Al-Baqarah: 186	Surah Al-Qiyamah: 2	Surah Taha: 1-2
Surah Al-Baqarah: 222	Surah An-Nahl: 114	Surah Yunus: 58
Surah Al-Baqarah: 243	Surah An-Nahl: 120-1	
Surah Al-Baqarah: 251	Surah An-Nahl: 14	
Surah Al-Baqarah: 269	Surah An-Nahl: 18	
Surah Al-Bayyinah: 8	Surah An-Nahl: 78	
Surah Al-Fajr: 1-2	Surah An-Naml: 40	

Hadith References:

In a Hadith narrated by Abu Hurairah ﷺ, Rasulullah ﷺ said, the best fast after Ramadan, is in the month of Allah ﷻ, Muharram; and the best prayer after the obligatory prayer (fard) is the night prayer, qiyam ul layl. (Sahih Muslim: 1163)

In a Hadith, narrated by Abu Darda ﷺ, Rasulullah ﷺ mentioned that there are two angels that record and pray for people if they give for the sake of Allah ﷻ that whatever they give to be replaced by something even better, and for those who are stingy, to allow what they have saved for themselves to go to waste.

In an authentic Hadith in Sahih al-Bukhari (1403) it is narrated that when Hakeem ﷺ came to Madinah, he asked Rasulullah ﷺ for money on numerous occasions, and Rasulullah ﷺ fulfilled his request each time.

The Hadith continues: "Whoever receives money and has a generous heart, Allah ﷻ will put *khair* in what he receives. However, whoever takes with greed will never have any *khair* in what they take…"

The Hadith continues: "For the one whose heart has greed, he will keep eating but will never be full…"

The Hadith continues to tell us about the long life of Hakeem ﷺ, in which Syedina Abu Bakr ﷺ attempted to give him a share of the bounty the Muslims had received, to which Hakeem ﷺ refused. Hadhrat Omar ﷺ tried to give him a share of the bounty, but Hakeem ﷺ refused. Syedina Omar ﷺ, being a person known for his justice, at the response of Hakeem ﷺ rose on the pulpit and proclaimed "Oh Muslims, know that I gave him his rights and he chose not to take it."

Hadith "Having a good thought of Allah ﷻ is by itself having the best form of ibadat," (Imam al-Hakim) and mentioned for us to "renew our *iman*." (Imam Ahmad) "*dua* is ibadat itself" (narrated in an authentic Hadith by Nu'man ibn Bashir ﷺ)

As we know from the Hadith that no ones *iman* can be complete unless they love Rasulullah ﷺ more than their money, their children and all of creation

And in a Hadith narrated by Imam Bukhari ﷺ, Abu Hurraira ﷺ said that Rasulullah ﷺ said that between one Umrah and another Umrah, Allah ﷻ forgives all sins between them. In another Hadith it is mentioned that those who go to *Hajj* and *Umrah* are the guests of Allah ﷻ, and Allah ﷻ made it compulsory upon Himself to honor His guests.

- In a Hadith narrated by Imam Tirmidhi ﷺ, Rasulullah ﷺ said to keep doing *Hajj* and *Umrah*, as it removes poverty by gaining the forgiveness of Allah ﷻ; and Rasulullah ﷺ completed four Umrahs during.

- In a Hadith narrated by Abdullah ibn Omar ﷺ, Rasulullah ﷺ said in every step of tawaf you receive a reward and a sin is removed, as narrated by Imams Ahmad, Tirmidhi, Hakim and ibn Khuzayma ﷺ.

Rasulullah ﷺ said in a Hadith "Oh people, ask Allah's ﷻ forgiveness, verily I ask 70 times a day," and in some narrations 100 times a day.

Astaghfirullah al-'Adheemal-ladhi la ilaha illa Huwal-Hayyul-Qayyum wa atubu ilaih

I seek the forgiveness of Allah the Most Great, Whom there is none worthy except Him, the Living, The Eternal, and I repent unto Him ﷻ.

In a Hadith narrated by Imam Tirmidhi, anyone who makes the above astaghfar, Allah ﷻ forgives him or her from even the major sins.

in a Hadith, the closest to him are those with the best of characters. Also, in a Hadith narrated by Imam Ahmad ﷺ, Rasulullah ﷺ said that the perfect *iman* of a mumin is such that he has a great character, is humble, and he loves people and people love him; and there is no *khair* in someone who does not love people and people do not love him.

In a Hadith, Rasulullah ﷺ said that Allah ﷻ is the Most Shy, and the Most Covering of others faults. In another Hadith, Rasulullah ﷺ said that Allah ﷻ is the Most Shy and the Most Generous. He is the Most Shy when His slave raises his hands, as He is shy to return them back empty handed. Normally it is the one who asks that is shy! How wonderful a situation we are in!

In a Hadith, Hadhrat Omar ﷺ recounts that Rasulullah ﷺ said that any Muslim that can bring a witness on the Day of Judgement will enter *Jannah*! The Sahaba ﷺ, asked the question (what a mercy their questions are for us!) that what if someone is unable to bring four witnesses, Rasulullah ﷺ replied that they could bring three; the Sahaba ﷺ then asked if they were unable to bring three, and Rasulullah ﷺ responded by saying that they could bring two, and the Sahaba ﷺ became shy to ask any further. (Sahih Bukhari 1368)

In a Hadith, Rasulullah ﷺ also said "In some poetry there is wisdom," encouraging believers to find wisdom wherever it may be.

In a Hadith, Rasulullah ﷺ said the worst of people on the Day of Judgement are those who are avoided out of fear for their tongues.

In Sahih Bukhari, Rasulullah ﷺ mentioned in a hadith that he is the most pious and knows Allah ﷻ the most ﷺ!

Saying this, we find in another hadith narrated by Mughira ibn Shu'ba, that Rasulullah ﷺ used to stand in prayer for such long hours that his feet became swollen. The Sahaba ﷺ asked Rasulullah ﷺ why he stood in prayer, since Allah ﷻ has forgiven for what has past and for what is to come, and Rasulullah ﷺ responded, "Should I not be a grateful slave of Allah ﷻ?" Ya Syedi ﷺ Ya Rasulullah ﷺ!

Rasulullah ﷺ said to the Sahaba in a Hadith narrated in Sahih Muslim: "Should I not tell you of that which deletes your bad deeds and elevates you in *Jannah*? To make *wudu* despite the weather/circumstances, to walk to the *masjid*, and to wait for the next *salah* after performing *salah*." If the weather is cold, or the circumstances difficult, there is a way to get closer to Allah ﷻ! To do *wudu* and, as a result, your sleep to go away is better for you than for your *ruh* to go away without praying!

In a Hadith narrated in ibn Majah and by Imam Ahmad ﷺ, Abu Hurrairah ﷺ narrates that Rasulullah ﷺ used to love optimism. Hence, we must content and happy.

In a Hadith narrated in Abu Dawud and by Imam Ahmad ﷺ, ibn Dalaimi ﷺ mentions that he had some issues in his heart regarding the acceptance of the qadr of Allah ﷻ, and he was finding it hard to accept, so he went to ask Ubay in Kab ﷺ. In answering the concerns of ibn Dalaimi ﷺ, Ubay ibn Kaab ﷺ said:

"If Allah ﷻ were to punish the people of the heavens (meaning the angels) and earth, this would be more than they deserve, and if He were to be Kind and Merciful, that which He is, that is more than they deserve. If a mountain of gold the size of Uhud were spent for the sake of Allah ﷻ, it would not be accepted unless one believes in the qadr of Allah ﷻ. What is meant for you will never be missed, and what has been missed was never meant for you."

Ibn Dalaimi ﷺ then went to Abdullah ibn Masud ﷺ and asked about the qadr, and he mentioned what Ubay ibn Kaab ﷺ mentioned. Ibn Dalaimi ﷺ then went to Hudaifah ibn al Yaman ﷺ, and he mentioned what Abdullah ibn Masud ﷺ had mentioned about qadr. Ibn Dulaimi ﷺ then went to Zayd ibn Thabit ﷺ, and he mentioned what Hudaifah ibn al Yaman ﷺ had mentioned regarding qadr.

In a Hadith narrated by ibn Abbas ﷺ, Rasulullah ﷺ said that "The best days that Allah ﷻ loves good deeds the most in are these days, meaning the ten days of Dhul Hijjah." (Abu Dawud 2438)

And in a Hadith narrated by Syedina Jabir ؓ, Rasulullah ﷺ said: "[of] the ten best days, the tenth is the day of sacrifice (Adha), and the uneven numbered day is the day of Arafah, and these are the ten days of Dhul Hijjah." (Imam Ahmad)

And in another Hadith, Syedina Jabir ؓ narrates that Rasulullah ﷺ said that there are "no days better than the ten days of Dhul Hijjah." (ibn Hibban 3853)

In a Hadith, the Sahaba ؓ asked Rasulullah ﷺ if the mujahid could compare to the one who worships in these ten days, to which Rasulullah ﷺ responded that no one can compare to the person who worships in these ten days except for the mujahid who gives away everything he owns and takes what remains with him and leaves it all on the battlefield, including his life. Only this person can compare to the one who worships in these ten days!

- In a Hadith narrated by Abdullah ibn Omar ؓ, Rasulullah ﷺ said that there are no days in the year that are greater, and Allah ﷻ loves good deeds in these days (Imam Ahmad)

- In a Hadith, Aisha ؓ narrates that Rasulullah ﷺ said: "There is no other day that Allah ﷻ frees more slaves from jahannaum than the day of Arafah! Allah ﷻ says to His angels on that day, 'Look at My slaves!'" (Muslim 3288)

- Yaum un-Nahr: The day of Eid ul Adha, in a Hadith it is mentioned as the best day of the year

In a Hadith, Rasulullah ﷺ said there are four types of people:

1) *Those with a good intention who do not complete the action they intended; they will be rewarded for their good intention*

2) *Those with a good intention who complete the action they intended; they will be rewarded for their intention and the action*

3) *Those with a bad intention but who do not commit the action they intended; they will be rewarded for their inaction*

4) *Those with a bad intention who do commit the action they intended; they will be accounted for their action*

Nawafil: try to do as many *nawafil salah* as you can, as it is a mentioned in a Hadith that a person's maqam is raised and that bad deeds are erased with each *sujood*.

Fasting: Fast as much as you can. It is mentioned in a Hadith, when a companion asked what the best of deeds was, Rasulullah ﷺ said to fast.

Rasulullah ﷺ said in a Hadith that there are moments of inspiration and baraka, so make the most of them! (narrated by Syed Muhammad ibn Maslamah, At-Tabarani: 2398)

As Allah ﷻ said in a Hadith Qudsi: "I am as my slave thinks of Me, so let my slave think of Me as they want."

In fact in another Hadith, narrated in Muslim: "No one should die except with having a good thought of Allah ﷻ."

In a Hadith, narrated by Abdullah ibn Masud ؓ, Rasulullah ﷺ said anyone who has even half of an atom of arrogance in their heart will not enter *jannah*.

In a Hadith, narrated by Abbas ibn Rabiah ؓ, Rasulullah ﷺ said whoever is humble towards Allah ﷻ, Allah ﷻ will raise; the humble one is that who believes he is the lowest, and in the eyes of others he is actually the greatest. If a person is arrogant, Allah ﷻ will lower him no matter where he is, and people will see him lowly as well. (Musnad Shihab)

In a Hadith narrated by Abu Hurrairah ﷺ, Rasulullah ﷺ wanted to buy trousers, and the owner of the shop wanted to kiss the blessed hands of Rasulullah ﷺ, but Rasulullah ﷺ said this is for kings! Abu Hurrairah ﷺ wanted to carry the things of Rasulullah ﷺ but Rasulullah ﷺ said people should carry their own things.

And as Rasulullah ﷺ said, whoever is not thankful to the people, he is not thankful to Allah ﷻ [at-Tirmidhi], I would like to thank you very much and jazakAllah *khair* for your *duas*, patience, condolences and for standing by us.

Rasulullah ﷺ said regarding this, that there is a polish for everything that takes away rust, and the polish for the heart is the remembrance of Allah ﷻ. (Al-Bukhari)

However, after a certain number of times (in some narrations 3, in others left open), Rasulullah ﷺ said, "Ya Hakeem! Verily this money is sweet and green…"

Hadith narrated by Imam Bukhari ﷺ, Abu Hurraira ﷺ said that Rasulullah ﷺ said that between one Umrah and another Umrah, Allah ﷻ forgives all sins between them. In another Hadith it is mentioned that those who go to *Hajj* and *Umrah* are the guests of Allah ﷻ, and Allah ﷻ made it compulsory upon Himself to honor His guests.

When Syeda Ayesha ﷺ was going for Umrah, Rasulullah ﷺ said to her, you will get the reward according to what you spend and according to your effort, as narrated by Imam Hakim ﷺ.

Poem References:

An Arab Bedouin, came to Rasulullah ﷺ and said: "Oh the Messenger of Allah ﷺ ! We have come to you, and in our midst there is no camel that is fit nor a baby that is quiet!" The bedouin then sang a poem:

"We do not have anyone to run to save You,

And where would people run to other than to the Messenger!"

Rasulullah ﷺ went to the mimbar (pulpit) with his clothes dragging on the floor. Rasulullah ﷺ , upon reaching, said: "Oh Allah ﷻ ! Shower us with what is mentioned in the hadith. Then Rasulullah ﷺ praised Allah ﷻ) and made dua.

In the hadith, Rasulullah ﷺ said: "If Abu Talib was to be alive, he would have been happy to see this. Who will recite to us what he said?" Ali ؓ stood up and said: "Oh Rasulullah ﷺ, are you referring to his (Abu Talib) saying:

That fair complexioned one, (referring to Rasulullah ﷺ) by whose face the prayer for rain is sought, He is the caretaker of orphans, and is the guardian of widows;

The family of Bani Hashim will seek refuge in him, and, under Him, they are in Mercy and Great Virtue.

[I swear], by my life, I have been occupied by the love of Ahmad and his brothers (his children); an occupation of continuous love.

Who is like him! If his virtues were compared and judged against those who people seek from;

Wise, Guided, Just, and never the oppressor; he is guarded by a Lord who is never heedless of him!

Generous towards all! He is Glorious and descends from Glory, a firm inheritance in Glory that does not waver!

And the Lord of Creation has supported him with His victory, and he has manifested a religion that will never disappear,

And they knew that our son is not considered a liar by us and he is not concerned by those who say otherwise,

He became praised amongst our entire honored lineage; no matter who competes they will end up short!

I have protected him with my life, defended him by my shield and by my people."

Fath ul Bari (v2, Pg 575) – ibn Hajr ﷺ

وابيض يستسقى الغمام بوجهه

عن أنسٍ قال: جاء رجلٌ أعرابيٌّ إلى النبيِّ صلى الله عليه وسلم فقال: يا رسولَ الله أَتَيْناك وما لنا بعيرُ يَئِطُّ ، ولا صبيٌّ يغط ثم أنشدَه شعرًا يقولُ فيه   وليس لنا إلا إليك فرارُنا . وأين فرارُ الناسِ إلا إلى الرسلِ ، فقام يجرُّ رداءَه حتى صعِدَ المنبرَ فقال: اللهمَّ اسقِنا الحديث وفيه ثم قال صلى الله عليه وسلم : لو كان أبو طالبٍ حيًّا لقرَّتْ عيناه. من ينشدُنا قولَه ؟ فقام عليٌّ فقال: يا رسولَ الله ، كأنك أردتَ قولَه وأبيضَ يُسْتَسقى الغمامُ بوجهِه الأبيات

الراوي: مسلم الملائي المحدث: ابن حجر العسقلاني- المصدر: فتح الباري لابن حجر   الصفحة أو الرقم: 2/575

خلاصة حكم المحدث: فيه ضعف لكنه يصلح للمتابعة

وأبيضُ يستسقي الغمــــــام بوجهه ٭
ثمــــــــــــالِ اليتامى عصــــمةٍ للأرامل

يلوذُ به الهلاك مــــــــــن آل هاشمٍ ٭
فهم عنده في رحــــــــــــــمةٍ وفواضل

لعمري لقد كلفِّـــــــــــتُ وجداً بأحمد ٭
وإخوته دأب المحــــــــبِّ المواصـــــــــل

فمن مثلُه في النـــــاس أي مؤمَّل ٭
إذا قاســـــــــــه الحكَّـــــــــام عند التفاضل

حليمُ رشيد عادل غــــــــير طائش ٭
يوالي إلــــــــهاً ليـــــــــــس عنه بغافل

كريمُ المساعي مـــــاجدٌ وابن ماجد ٭
له إرثُ مجدٍ ثابـــــــــــتٍ غير ناصــــــــــل

وأيَّده ربُّ العباد بنصــــــــــره ٭
وأظهر دينـــــــــــــاً حقـــه غير زائل

لقد علموا أن ابننا لا مكــــــــــذبُ ٭
لدينا ولا يعنـــــــــــــــى بقولِ الأباطل

فأصبح فينا أحمــــــــــدُ في أرومةٍ ٭
يقصر عنها ســــــــــــــــورةُ المتطاول

حدبت بنفسي دونـــــــــه وحميته ٭
ودافعت عــــــــــــــــنه بالذَّرى والكلاكل

In a narration, Al Abbas ﷺ saw Abu Lahab, in hellfire, and he asked him, *"What have you encountered?"* Abu Lahab said: *"I have not found any rest since I left you, except that I have been given water to drink in this (the space between his thumb and other fingers) and that is because of my manumitting of Thuwaiba."*

Imam Jamaluddin al Qasimi al Dimashqi ﷺ said:

If this is the state of the disbeliever who has been cursed with *"tabbat yada"* for eternity in hellfire,

And we are told that his torture is reduced every Monday due to this happiness upon the birth of Ahmad ﷺ,

So what about the one who whose life is happy by Ahmad ﷺ and who died in *iman*?

قال العباسِ رضي الله عنه أنه رآه [أي أبو لهب] في منامِه بعد موتِه - يجولُ في شرِّ حالٍ فقال له ما لقيت بعدكم راحةً إلا أن العذابَ يخففُ عني كلَّ يومِ اثنينِ وفي لفظٍ غيرَ أني سقيت في هذه أشار إلى النقرةِ التي تحت إبهامِه وفي آخرٍ وأشار إلى النقرةِ التي بين الإبهامِ والتي تليها وذلك لأن النبيَّ صلى اللهُ عليهِ وسلَّم ولد يومَ الاثنينِ وكانت ثويبةُ بشرت أبا لهبٍ بمولدِه صلى اللهُ عليهِ وسلَّم فأعتقَها (١)

وقد رُؤي أبو لهب بعد موتِه في النوم فقيل له ما حالك؟ قال: في النار، إلا أنه خفف عني كل ليلة اثنين، وأمص من بين أصبعي هاتين ماءً، وأشار برأسِ أصبعه وأن ذلك بإعتاقي لثويبة عندما بشرتني بولادة النبي صلى الله عليه وسلم وبإرضاعها له (٢)

إذا كـان هـذا كافـر جـاء ذمـةٌ ٭ وتثبت يداه في الجحيم مخـلـدا
أتـى أنـه في يوم الاثنيـن دائمـاً ٭ يخفف عنه بالسرور بأحمــدا
فما الظن بالعبد الذي كان عمره ٭ بأحمد مسروراً ومات موحـدا

---

(١) الامام السخاوي الأجوبة المرضية   الصفحة   737/2
(٢) شرح الزرقاني على المواهب اللدنيه بالمنح المحمدية
1/260

Al Ajwiba al Mardiya (v2, Pg 737) – As Sakahwi
Sahih al Bukhari (v7, Book 62, No. 38)
Explanation of Al Muwahib al Laduniya (v1, Pg 260) – al Zurqani

The River of Light

Rasulullah's ﷺ uncle Al Abbas ؓ said to him: "O Messenger of Allah, I wish to praise you." Rasulullah ﷺ replied: "Go ahead - may Allah ﷻ adorn your mouth with silver!" He said:

Before you came to this world

you were blessed in the shadows and in the repository (i.e. loins)
in the time when they (Adam and Eve) covered themselves with leaves.
Then you descended to the earth,
neither as a human being, nor as a piece of flesh, nor as a clot,
But as a drop that boarded the ark
when the flood destroyed the eagle and the rest of the idols:
A drop that progressed from the loins to the wombs
in the succession of the worlds and the heavens
Until the Preserver of All made your immense honor issue in the highest summit of the line of Khindif.
And then, when you were born, a light rose over the earth until it illuminated the horizon with its radiance.
We are in that illumination
and that original light and those paths of guidance -- and thanks to them pierce through.

قال العباس بن عبد المطلب يارسول الله اريد ان امتدحك فقال : قل ،
لا يفضض الله فاك . فقال العباس رضي الله عنه

من قبلها طبت في الظلال وفي مستودع حيث يخصف الورق
ثم هبطت البلاد لا بشر انت ولامضغة ولا علق
بل نطفة تركب السفين وقد ألجم نسرا واهله الغرق
تنقل من صالب الى رحم اذا مضى عالم بدا طبق
حتى احتوى بيتك المهيمن من خندف علياء تحتها النطق

Translation source: www.livingislam.org

142

Once the prophet ﷺ was sitting in a room with Aisha and fixing his shoes. It was very warm, and Aisha looked to his blessed forehead and noticed that there were beads of sweat on it. She became overwhelmed by the majesty of that sight was staring at him long enough for him to notice. He said, *"What's the matter?"* She replied, *"If Abu Kabir Al-Huthali, the poet, saw you, he would know that his poem was written for you."* The Prophet ﷺ asked, *"What did he say?"* She replied, "Abu Kabir said:

'that if you looked to the majesty of the moon, it twinkles and lights up the world for everybody to see."

So the Prophet ﷺ got up, walked to Aisha, kissed her between the eyes, and said, *"Wallahi ya Aisha, you are like that to me and more."*

في رواية: عن عائشة قالت: كان رسول الله صلى الله عليه وسلم يخصف نعله وكنت أغزل فنظرت إلى رسول الله صلى الله عليه وسلم فجعل جبينه يعرق وجعل عرقه يتولد نورا قالت فبهت فيه فنظرت إلى رسول الله صلى الله عليه وسلم فقال ما لك بهت فقلت يا رسول الله نظرت إليك فجعل جبينك يعرق وجعل عرقك يتولد نورا فلو رآك أبو كبير الهذلي لعلم أنك أحق بشعره قال وما يقول يا عائشة أبو كبير الهذلي فقالت: يقول:

وَمُبَرَّاً مِنْ كُلِّ غُبَّرِ حَيْضَةٍ ۞ وَفَسَادِ مُرْضِعَةٍ وَدَاءٍ مُغِيلِ

فَإِذَا نَظَرْتَ إِلَى أَسِرَّةِ وَجْهِهِ   بَرَقَتْ كَبَرْقِ الْعَارِضِ الْمُتَهَلِّلِ

وفي رواية: عَنْ عَائِشَةَ رَضِيَ اللهُ عَنْهَا قَالَتْ: كُنْتُ قَاعِدَةً أَغْزِلُ وَالنَّبِيُّ – صلى الله عليه وسلم – يَخْصِفُ نَعْلَهُ فَجَعَلَ جَبِينُهُ يَعْرَقُ وَجَعَلَ عَرَقُهُ يَتَوَلَّدُ نُورًا فَبُهِتُّ فَنَظَرَ إِلَىَّ رَسُولُ اللهِ – صلى الله عليه وسلم – فَقَالَ: مَا لَكِ يَا عَائِشَةُ بُهِتِّ؟. قُلْتُ: جَعَلَ جَبِينُكَ يَعْرَقُ وَجَعَلَ عَرَقُكَ يَتَوَلَّدُ نُورًا وَلَوْ رَآكَ أَبُو كَبِيرٍ الْهُذَلِىُّ لَعَلِمَ أَنَّكَ أَحَقٌّ بِشِعْرِهِ. قَالَ: وَمَا يَقُولُ أَبُو كَبِيرٍ؟. قَالَتْ قُلْتُ: يَقُولُ

وَمُبَرَّاً مِنْ كُلِّ غُبَّرِ حَيْضَةٍ ۞ وَفَسَادِ مُرْضِعَةٍ وَدَاءٍ مُغِيلِ

في رواية: عن عائشة قالت: كان رسول الله صلى الله عليه وسلم يخصف نعله وكنت أغزل فنظرت إلى رسول الله صلى الله عليه وسلم فجعل جبينه يعرق وجعل عرقه يتولد نورا قالت فبهت فيه فنظرت إلى رسول الله صلى الله عليه وسلم فقال ما لك بهت فقلت يا رسول الله نظرت إليك فجعل جبينك يعرق وجعل عرقك يتولد نورا فلو رآك أبو كبير الهذلي لعلم أنك أحق بشعره قال وما يقول يا عائشة أبو كبير الهذلي فقالت: يقول:

وَمُبَرَّإٍ مِنْ كُلِّ غُبَّرِ حَيْضَةٍ ۞ وَفَسَادِ مُرْضِعَةٍ وَدَاءٍ مُغِيلِ

فَإِذَا نَظَرْتَ إِلَى أَسِرَّةِ وَجْهِهِ   بَرَقَتْ كَبَرْقِ الْعَارِضِ الْمُتَهَلِّلِ

وفي رواية: عَنْ عَائِشَةَ رَضِيَ اللهُ عَنْهَا قَالَتْ: كُنْتُ قَاعِدَةً أَغْزِلُ وَالنَّبِيُّ - صلى الله عليه وسلم - يَخْصِفُ نَعْلَهُ فَجَعَلَ جَبِينُهُ يَعْرَقُ وَجَعَلَ عَرَقُهُ يَتَوَلَّدُ نُورًا فَبُهِتُّ فَنَظَرَ إِلَى رَسُولِ اللهِ - صلى الله عليه وسلم - فَقَالَ: مَا لَكِ يَا عَائِشَةُ بُهِتِّ؟ قُلْتُ   جَعَلَ جَبِينَكَ يَعْرَقُ وَجَعَلَ عَرَقُكَ يَتَوَلَّدُ نُورًا وَلَوْ رَآكَ أَبُو كَبِيرٍ الْهُذَلِيُّ لَعَلِمَ أَنَّكَ أَحَقُّ بِشِعْرِهِ. قَالَ: وَمَا يَقُولُ أَبُو كَبِيرٍ؟. قَالَتْ قُلْتُ: يَقُولُ

وَمُبَرَّإٍ مِنْ كُلِّ غُبَّرِ حَيْضَةٍ ۞ وَفَسَادِ مُرْضِعَةٍ وَدَاءٍ مُغِيلِ

فَإِذَا نَظَرْتَ إِلَى أَسِرَّةِ وَجْهِهِ ۞ بَرَقَتْ كَبَرْقِ الْعَارِضِ الْمُتَهَلِّلِ

قَالَتْ فَقَامَ إِلَيَّ النَّبِيُّ - صلى الله عليه وسلم - وَقَبَّلَ بَيْنَ عَيْنَيَّ وَقَالَ: جَزَاكِ اللهُ يَا عَائِشَةُ عَنِّي خَيْرًا مَا سُرِرْتِ مِنِّي كَسُرُورِي مِنْكِ.

الحافظ المزي : تهذيب الكمال – الصفحة :
Al-Hafiz Almizi - Tahtheeb Al Kamal 18/276

Biographical Index

Khadijah ؓ	Said ibn Jubayr ؓ
Imam Ali ؓ	Abbas ibn Rabiah ؓ
Imam Hasan ؓ	Hafiz Shamsuddin Sakhawi ؒ
Syedina Bilal ؓ	Imam Ahmad ؒ
Abdullah bin Zubair ؓ	Fudhail ibn Iyad ؒ
Omar ؓ	Baba Mohammed Said ؒ
Abu Hurairah ؓ	Imam ibn Abi Dunya ؒ
Abu Bakr ؓ	Abu Hazim ibn Dinar ؒ
Abu Qatada ؓ	Abu Qulaba ؒ
Said al Khudri ؓ	Muhammad ibn Abdullah ؒ
Abdullah ibn Masud ؓ	Abdullah ibn Zaid ؒ
Muadh ؓ	Shaykh Abdul Qadir Jilani ؒ
Zaid ibn Haritha ؓ	Sidi Shaykh Hamid ؒ
Anas ؓ	Zakariyya ؏
Abu Darda ؓ	Yusuf ؏
Abu Quhafa ؓ	Ibrahim ؏
Aisha ؓ	Abu Hazim ibn Dinar ؒ
Abdullah ibn Abbas ؓ	Ayub ؏
Hakeem ibn Huzaim ibn Khuwalyd ؓ	Yunus ؏
Hadhrat Uthman ؓ	Yaqub ؏
Nu'man ibn Bashir ؓ	Musa ؏

Hasan al Basri ﷜	Isa ﷵ
Abdullah ibn Omar ﷜	Jibreel ﷵ
Syedina Jabir ﷜	Mariam ﷵ
Ubay in Kab ﷜	Suleiman ﷵ
Ibn Dalaimi ﷜	Daud ﷵ
Hudaifah ibn al Yaman ﷜	Syeda Hajr ﷵ
Zayd ibn Thabit ﷜	Yusuf ﷵ
Ibn Hajr ﷜	Sahaba ﷜
Abdullah ibn Salam ﷜	Ansar ﷜
Nuh ﷵ